Unless Recalled Earlier

At Work in
the Atomic City

At Work in the Atomic City

A Labor and Social History
of Oak Ridge, Tennessee

Russell B. Olwell

THE UNIVERSITY OF TENNESSEE PRESS / KNOXVILLE

LIBRARY OF CONGRESS CATALOGING-IN-PUBLICATION DATA

Olwell, Russell B., 1969–
 At work in the atomic city: a labor and social history of Oak Ridge,
 Tennessee / Russell B. Olwell.—1st ed.
  p. cm.
 Includes bibliographical references and index.
 ISBN 1-57233-324-3 (hardcover: acid-free paper)
 1. Oak Ridge National Laboratory—Employees. 2. Nuclear weapons
industry—Tennessee—Employees. 3. Oak Ridge National Laboratory—
History. I. Title.
HD8039.A62U434 2004
331.7'62345119'0976873—dc22   2004005732

To Mary and Laurea Lucy

Contents

Illustrations

Acknowledgments

Many people have conspired to make this project emerge as a book. Chris Appy, my graduate school advisor, encouraged this project from the beginning and has continued to do so. Charles Weiner, Deborah Fitzgerald, and Roe Smith also provided encouragement and hard questions to shape this work.

Archivists such as Marjorie Charlante and Charles Reeves at NARA provided vital help, often on short notice. I hope they realize that without them, no real research on this topic would ever make it to print. Archivists at other institutions, such as the Southern Labor History Archives at Georgia State University, Atlanta, have also helped me a great deal, and I owe Ben Primer, Princeton University archivist, for introducing me to the topics and techniques I use to this day.

Two major oral history collections made this work possible. Charles Jackson and Charles Johnson were gracious enough to lend me tapes from their work in Oak Ridge in the 1970s, and Stan Goldberg's video histories at the Smithsonian captured testimony that would have never been taken otherwise. All scholars of Oak Ridge and World War II owe these men gratitude for their work and their generosity to other scholars in the field.

Scholars in this field have been gracious in providing comments and advice. Gil Whittemore and Robert Proctor were helpful on health issues, and the comments and work of Bart Hacker and J. Samuel Walker forced me to clarify my thinking on the issues of patriotism, health, and safety.

Throughout the process of making this dissertation a book, Robert Zieger has been a combination of supportive and critical that I believe helped the book immeasurably.

I dedicate this book to my wife and daughter. Howard Zinn has written that we must be human beings first and historians second, something I understand better as a result of having Mary Wright and Laurea Lucy Olwell Wright in my life.

Abbreviations

AEC	Atomic Energy Commission
AFL	American Federation of Labor
ATLC	Atomic Trades and Labor Council (AFL)
AWOC	Atomic Workers Organizing Committee
C&CCC	Carbon and Carbide Chemical Corporation
CIO	Congress of Industrial Organizations
DOE	Department of Energy
FEPC	Fair Employment Practices Commission
FMCS	Federal Mediation and Conciliation Service
IAM	International Association of Machinists
IBEW	International Brotherhood of Electrical Workers
K-25	Gaseous Diffusion Plant, Oak Ridge
MED	Manhattan Engineer District
NCRP	National Committee on Radiation Protection
NLRB	National Labor Relations Board
TEC	Tennessee Eastman Corporation
TVA	Tennessee Valley Authority
UGCCWU	United Gas Coke and Chemical Workers (CIO)
UMW	United Mine Workers Union (IND)
WMC	War Manpower Commission
X-10	Research Laboratory and Reactor, Oak Ridge
Y-12	Electromagnetic Separation Plant, Oak Ridge

CHAPTER 1

The Birth of Oak Ridge

IN SEPTEMBER 1942, Gen. Leslie Groves looked out on sparsely populated farmland tucked between two ridges and saw the area that would become known as Oak Ridge. He chose the site for its proximity to rail lines, safe distance from the coast, and high ridges, which promised to muffle that the sound of any accidental explosion. He named the area Clinton Engineer Works, a code name for the facility that would help build the atomic bomb. Within months, the site was swarming with construction equipment and workers. These men and machines built four facilities—totaling over four hundred buildings—to process atomic materials for the Manhattan Project. By 1943, the companies that operated the plants were hiring and training thousands to work the dials and valves of the electromagnetic and chemical machinery that separated isotopes of uranium, the explosive chemicals in the atomic bombs.[1]

Oak Ridge formed one piece of a vast production network, an important link in the atomic assembly line. The best-known site, Los Alamos, served as the scientific center of the project, where physicists and mathematicians designed the bombs and assembled their final components. At another familiar site, the Chicago Metallurgical Laboratory, physicists and chemists created the world's first self-sustaining nuclear reaction beneath the University of Chicago's Stagg Field. While these two facilities are well documented in popular and scholarly works, Hanford, Washington, and Oak Ridge, Tennessee—the production facilities of the Manhattan Project —are less well known. At these two sites, engineers, scientists, and workers processed the materials that would form the core of the bomb.

At Oak Ridge, great factory buildings separated two uranium isotopes, U-235 from U-238, to synthesize the explosive for the atomic bomb dropped on Hiroshima. Oak Ridge played a critical role in the Manhattan Project, processing uranium into explosive material for a working nuclear device. Uranium mined in the Belgian Congo and Canada was first milled and then brought to Oak Ridge. In the gaseous diffusion plant (code named K-25), uranium was combined with fluorine and pumped through a thin metal barrier that separated U-235 from U-238. The product was brought to the electromagnetic separation plant (code named Y-12), where it was refined in cyclotrons to further separate the isotopes, leaving a residue of U-235 for use in the bomb. At Clinton Laboratories (code named X-10), scientists and engineers processed tons of uranium to create a few grams of the artificial element plutonium, a pilot for the full-scale production of plutonium at Hanford.

From the founding of Oak Ridge, the U.S. Army set a breakneck schedule for uranium and plutonium production, requiring a vast recruiting and training effort. The great factory facilities were quickly designed and assembled by a number of contractors, especially J. A. Jones Construction, using a small army of skilled construction workers. Speed alone counted for nothing, as the wiring and plumbing for each facility needed to be exact to avoid spoiling the scarce product. In addition, the entire facility required careful maintenance and cleaning, necessitating another workforce. To house, feed, transport, and keep house for the workers, the army contracted with a separate company, Roane-Anderson.

The search for men and women to perform these jobs during the war was a Herculean task. Workers were recruited throughout the nation: skilled trades workers brought by train from New York, unskilled laborers lured out of the cotton fields and lumber mills of Alabama onto trucks, coal miners drawn from Appalachia to work in the atomic factories, all looking for a better way of life. Recruitment of workers for the Manhattan Project was given the highest priority during World War II's tight labor market, but it was still difficult to keep the operation fully manned. Hindering recruitment further, workers could be told only that they would be brought to Knoxville to work on a "government project," not the purpose of the facility, the job they were hired to do, or the exact location of their housing.

On arrival at Oak Ridge, the army told new recruits that they were working for the cause of freedom, but, paradoxically, these workers found themselves living in a military-base atmosphere. To exit or enter the city, residents passed through one of seven "gates," where badges were checked (even children had them) and cars were searched by military police. The plants had checkpoints and fences of their own to keep out all but their own employees. Within the three plants, the content and purpose of each job was a military secret. Element names—such as uranium, plutonium, and fluorine—were changed into code, with a different code system at each plant. Workers wore overalls of different colors and badges unique to their job. The army forbade them to discuss their jobs with fellow workers or family members. Outside the plants, badges could be checked at any time.

Oak Ridge was more than a link in the atomic chain, solely devoted to producing materials for the atomic bomb. It was also a community with tens of thousands of residents. Founded in wartime, Oak Ridge's original character more closely approximated a military base than the rural village that predated it. The army administered Oak Ridge without pretense of democracy, and for the duration of the war, it allowed no local elections, free press, or freedom of assembly. Because Oak Ridge was owned and managed by the U.S. Army, military work and civil society overlapped there, making it difficult to see where the former ended and the latter began. The army's security system created a "city behind a fence," a community developed in isolation from the rest of the country. Under these conditions, work in Oak Ridge took on a patriotic and military character that profoundly shaped life in the city.

Consolidation and Erosion of the Patriotic Consensus

The concept of workers as patriotic soldiers had an impact on the concept of citizenship during World War II, both in Oak Ridge and nationwide. Military service traditionally has been associated with temporary surrender of civil rights. Soldiers, unlike citizens, do not elect their leaders, nor do they have a right to disobey commands. They are required to comply with military security regulations and must not question the wisdom of the conflict at hand. Although they can be thrust into danger at a moment's notice, they have no right to avoid hazards of duty. Soldiers also do not have the right of free speech—especially if that speech might give away information useful to the enemy. As figure 1 shows, this code of conduct easily could be applied to the homefront, where even innocuous conversation or writing could be interpreted as a breach of security. During World War II, this curtailment of rights extended even to congressional debates over soldiers' enfranchisement, with many in Congress opposed to the vote for military personnel.[2]

The experience of work and community life during World War II created a public culture of patriotic consensus in Oak Ridge. By "patriotic consensus," I mean a civic culture that placed service to national defense goals above other competing values, such as civil liberties. This consensus had several key elements: a concept of workers as surrogate soldiers serving their nation, enforcement of secrecy restrictions about work at the facility, and

Oak Ridge was saturated with patriotic images such as this
propaganda poster, c. 1944. Box 20, Notebook 59,
RG 434-OR, Still Pictures Branch, NARA.

the prioritization of production speed over worker health and safety. This consensus was not monolithic, as workers and residents questioned some elements of military control from the start. These embedded rules set the parameters of much of Oak Ridge's civic history, limiting worker and community activism. If a resident questioned these rules—work, silence, and security—he or she ran the risk of being fired and evicted from the city.

This civic environment was not unique to Oak Ridge in the 1940s. Patriotic messages saturated World War II America, drawing parallels between service on the homefront and on the battlefield. Congressional proposals for national service drew on this metaphor, urging that workers be deterred from striking or even quitting a job. For the federal government, the issue of manpower at home became an extension of military command—a vast number of people needed to be recruited and deployed to areas of greatest need, then moved, housed, and fed to keep them in their factory foxholes. As the government and contractors built new facilities across the South, West, and Northwest, millions of men and women were deployed on an industrial and military frontier, from shipyards in Florida to steel mills in California. However, in Oak Ridge the identification of the city with national security was more direct than in other parts of the nation, as military necessity had given birth to the city itself.[3]

Throughout American history, completion of military service also has been used as leverage to bargain with the federal government for rights. In 1946–47, after the cessation of hostilities, soldiers returned home to Oak Ridge and labor unions stepped up their campaigns. The language of patriotism and sacrifice that the army used to recruit workers and to justify an intrusive security system now could be appropriated by workers and residents. Having been told to sacrifice for their country and the war effort, workers and union organizers couched their demands in terms of entitlement to civil, political, and labor rights based on patriotic sacrifices. During and after World War II, this language of patriotic protest served as a common touchstone for worker and community demands, as the army's main rhetorical tool was used to undermine its legitimacy. As the patriotic consensus started to crack, the community mobilized to gain freedom of the press, freedom of assembly, and the right to unionize.[4]

Within two years of postwar layoffs, the rumblings of the cold war were heard throughout the United States, and Oak Ridge became a vital defense institution once more. The security system built during World War II was reactivated and intensified during the cold war years, and the federal government once again told workers that they were soldiers, this time fighting world communism. Federal money flowed back into Oak Ridge, and the plants were put back on twenty-four-hour production.

Living at the heart of the conflict between the atomic superpowers, Oak Ridge's patriotic consensus re-cemented into place, surviving intact for decades. As Gary Gerstle and Ellen Schrecker have shown, the rise of anticommunism redefined "Americanism" in a more conservative and passive direction. The cold war transformed citizenship from positive activism to avoidance of unpatriotic behavior and thought. The ideology of anticommunism redefined allegiance in terms of defense against the Soviet Union and asked citizens voluntarily to relinquish political and civil rights. This sacrifice, however, did not give workers or community members the right to speak up in protest as it had during World War II, as dissent itself had been defined as unpatriotic. In world of enemies, international and domestic, anyone was suspect as an agent of the enemy, a fellow traveler, or a dupe of communism.

This cold war shift in discourse and thought hit workers and unions particularly hard. According to the Taft-Hartley Act of 1947, to strike or threaten a strike on a defense project was illegal and cause for presidential and judicial action against the union. All industries that affected national defense, and safety fell under this broad umbrella, even if the work being done was not of immediate defense importance. Defense workers and their unions were left virtually without recourse if negotiations deadlocked. For Oak Ridge's workers, these constraints were magnified, as no other field was considered more vital to the cold war than atomic material production.

National security also justified giving the military and, later, the Atomic Energy Commission (AEC), a free hand in running Oak Ridge. Exempt from congressional scrutiny during the war, and shielded by the power to classify documents indefinitely in the postwar years, information about production, health, safety, and the environment was off limits. In this atmosphere of secrecy, with no agency to check or balance those in charge, occupational and environmental health issues were minimized in order to maximize atomic production. Only with the end of the cold war in the 1980s did much of the information about health and environmental problems in the 1940s become available to researchers, workers, and residents of the area.

For workers at Oak Ridge, the "Good War," the cold war, and the fight for decent working conditions were intertwined. As one worker recently told a meeting with the Department of Energy's assistant secretary for environment, safety and health:

> I saw what these guys, the generation before me, went through. It was a war zone. They left the war in Europe, and they came back to K-25, and they faced another war of exposure from chemical agents, from transuranics, and things they never knew they were exposed to. They were told they could not talk about it. . . . These older guys that came off the farm and they hired back in the war, [it was] the first time in their life they could pay the mortgage on their farm, they could send junior to college, they had the first car that they could own, they could make their payments, they wanted that job and needed that job. . . . They did this through patriotism to their country. They were told they were fighting a cold war, they were told that this was a government facility. They were told to keep their mouth shut. They thought they were doing the right thing for their country. Now I call on my country to do the right thing for these sick workers and the widows that died. I am going to say, it was a worse war than Europe, and that's at K-25 in Oak Ridge.[5]

As the testimony above suggests, the experiences of workers at Oak Ridge during and after World War II raise many questions for historians. How could workers gain any control of their workplace under such strict security conditions? How did the situation at Oak Ridge change after the dropping of the atomic bomb? How did the union organizing drives at Oak Ridge in 1946 affect the plants and the community? How did postwar union negotiations change work at the plants? How safe was work in the plants and life in the community? While this book draws together information that has only recently been made public, the nature of this research means that it can offer partial answers to these questions. Any historian of Oak Ridge is confronted with a threefold problem: the classification of documents related to nuclear production, the code of silence surrounding the facility, and, tragically, the death of the city's founding generation.

Historiography

During the Manhattan Project, the army already had an eye to its future image, and it collected historical documents for preservation and ultimate use in writing the final account of the project. The U.S. Army, the AEC, and the Army Corps of Engineers have written their own official histories of Oak Ridge. These histories monumentalize the project and memorialize the administrative and managerial accomplishments of their agencies while downplaying the role of other agencies involved. They portray the project as an orderly, highly managed, and well-run endeavor, a tradition continued in biographies such as Robert S. Norris's *Racing for the Bomb*. In keeping with this patriotic theme, discussion of long-term health and environmental consequences of the project is absent. Official histories of the project's radiation safety standards, such as Barton Hacker's *Dragon's Tail* and J. Samuel Walker's *Permissible Dose*, depict Oak Ridge as a model of safety in spite of production pressures.[6]

Historians of science and technology have drawn from these official histories in their accounts and have expanded on them. Thomas Hughes, in his *Networks of Power*, places the Manhattan Project in the context of national technological development, along with such innovations as the Tennessee Valley Authority (TVA). Hughes cuts through the bravado of the official histories, but he does not address the history of workers on the project. Similarly, Peter Bacon Hales's *Atomic Spaces* provides a critical look at army policies on all three Manhattan Project sites through the lens of art history.

Community histories of Oak Ridge have taken a different approach to the subject by focusing on the grass-roots level instead of the city's huge, centrally driven technological system. Charles Jackson and Charles Johnson, in their *City Behind a Fence*, portray Oak Ridge as a place where people lived, worked, and built a community. Their work remains the most important account of Oak Ridge's civil development, particularly among the scientific and engineering elite of the city. In *These Are Our Voices,* writers from Oak Ridge told their own history, from the time before the plants were built until the present day.[7]

This book departs from previous scholarship in three ways. First, unlike official histories of the Manhattan Project, it treats Oak Ridge's workers and their experiences as central to the history of the project. The story of Oak Ridge's scientific, engineering, and managerial elite has been told ably in previous works, and I do not repeat it here.[8] Second, this work analyzes the community and the workplace as interconnected arenas of struggle at Oak Ridge: labor activism influenced the life of the community, and community activism enriched unionism. Prior studies have focused on either the community history or the work done within the plants, without drawing connections between the two. Finally, this book connects labor history with the history of science and medicine through analysis of occupational health and environmental issues in Oak Ridge. This history can inform recent federal programs created to compensate atomic workers for cancer and beryllium disease caused by Oak Ridge's working conditions. The examination presented here of federal occupational health policies in the 1940s demonstrates that present compensation policies are inadequate and dishonest.

In writing this book, I drew upon archival collections at the National Archives in College Park, Maryland, the National Archives Regional Branch in East Point, Georgia, the Public Reading Room at the Department of Energy's Oak Ridge Operation Office, and the Leo Goodman Papers at the Library of Congress, Manuscript Division. I conducted interviews with Oak Ridge residents, used interviews conducted by Charles Jackson and Charles Johnson in 1976–77, and relied upon a collection of video histories compiled by the late Stanley Goldberg in 1985. Freedom of Information Act requests yielded documents about accidents and health problems at the Oak Ridge facility. The Department of Energy (DOE) also has posted numerous documents and hearings on their Internet site, providing access to valuable materials on worker health and safety. Though no study of a site as vast as Oak Ridge can be called complete, I did my best to fit together all available pieces of the puzzle—ours is, after all, the last generation to have available both oral history subjects and documents. Though the next generation will have a more complete and well-organized documentary collection to draw from, they will have only cassettes and videotapes, and that will be an incalculable loss.

CHAPTER 2

Recruiting Workers

We are scraping the bottom of the barrel and the scrapings are not good.

—Tennessee Eastman Corporation, 1945

DURING WORLD WAR II, industrial recruitment for war production took on the fervor of a military campaign. Throughout the nation, the War Manpower Commission (WMC) launched campaigns, held rallies, scoured pool halls and bars, all to bring its message of patriotic labor to Americans. The message was simple: if Americans were to be victorious overseas, workers must serve in vital war industries. Patriotism meant working overtime, coming in on extra (or premium) days, and expending effort to "deliver the goods" to the troops in the field. The WMC urged workers to stay on the job, not to move on in search of higher wages, and not to break regulations by quitting, striking, or loafing. The commission was not entirely successful in its attempts to tap into worker (and employer) patriotism. Workers skipped out of jobs in search of higher pay, migrated north in search of better opportunities, and just plain disappeared. Employers also broke the rules of this system, hiring needed workers without WMC approval and "pirating" workers from other war industries when needed.

As Charles Chamberlain wrote in his book *Victory at Home*, "Federal recruitment and labor piracy opened new paths to social freedom and at least a modicum of economic democracy." His argument holds true for Oak Ridge's workers, white and African American, men and women.[1] The WMC successfully channeled many workers to important war work such as the Manhattan Project. Appealing to patriotism, as well as to workers' pocketbooks, the U.S. Army staffed the construction and production jobs required by the massive project. The WMC's carrot was a high wage—the stick was the threat of military draft. However, in order to bring workers to the site, the WMC, the army, and contractors made promises to workers, which workers took seriously in their decision to relocate. In return for labor on this patriotic project, workers believed that they would be rewarded, immediately or in the not-too-distant future, for their sacrifices.

Unlimited Demand for Workers

Gen. Leslie Groves knew from the start of the Manhattan Engineer District (MED, the official name of the Manhattan Project) that success depended on more than scientific brains and engineering expertise. It would require the skill and muscle of tens of thousands of construction workers, electricians, and production workers. The three sites chosen for the project— Hanford, Washington; Los Alamos, New Mexico; and what would become known as Oak Ridge, Tennessee—made the problem more difficult, as each was in a sparsely settled area with few established industries. However, Groves was convinced that the atomic bombs needed to be developed inland, far from the seacoasts, where it would be possible to maintain secrecy. With these factors in mind, Groves gave the necessary orders to bring workers from across the country to the Clinton Engineer Works. His initial estimates were conservative. Originally, he envisioned that the project would involve tens of thousands of workers. Eventually the project employed more than five hundred thousand, with, at its peak, eighty thousand construction workers and forty thousand production or factory workers in Oak Ridge at any one time.

Restrictions on wartime labor recruiting made fulfilling this manpower quota even more difficult, as industrial recruiters faced a frustrating system of constraints from federal agencies on what they could offer prospective employees. The WMC regulated recruiting practices by companies engaged in war work to prevent "labor piracy." The National War Labor Board (NWLB) held wage increases to the national price level to keep wartime inflation in check, and this restricted the ability of the Manhattan Project to recruit solely on the size of paychecks. The inability to offer higher wages threatened to doom efforts to recruit hundreds of thousands of workers to a remote location, northwest of Knoxville, where they would engage in difficult and tedious work.[2]

However, the Manhattan Project used other inducements to attract workers. First, the army and contractors, as a vital war industry, could defer the draft for workers in regions with labor shortages. This drew many who wished to avoid military service to war industries, an ironic way in which refugees from the front lines staffed this "patriotic" industry. One worker left Chattanooga for Oak Ridge upon learning from a friend who served on local draft board that he needed to find work in a war industry to avoid immediate service. When laid off from his job in a Chattanooga TNT plant, he recalled, recruiters "came to us and told us about work at Oak Ridge— that we would have a house." He was also promised that if he came to Oak Ridge, he would avoid overseas service, and if drafted, he would serve in uniform at Oak Ridge. Though both promises fell through, these incentives did their job—netting Oak Ridge one more worker at a time when every worker counted.[3]

Some workers came to Oak Ridge before or immediately after military service. One worker, who came to Oak Ridge while in high school, entered the service as soon as eligible. He recalled, "In 1944, the war was really at its peak, and I wanted to make sure I could get in. I wanted to get into the war before it was over. So in January 1945, I entered the Navy and stayed in a couple of years." This worker then returned to Oak Ridge to work, a pattern typical of many workers on the project whose service was a short interlude between stints of work at the plants.[4]

The project also circumvented federal recruiting restrictions by offering nonwage incentives to workers, including on-site housing in houses, dormitories and trailers, enough steady work for entire families to come to the site, and a good educational system for children. When necessary, Manhattan Project contractors disregarded governmental restrictions on "labor piracy" in order to bring African Americans, white agricultural workers, and women to Tennessee with promises of better jobs, higher pay, and increased job opportunities. To further attract workers to Oak Ridge, the army built thousands of housing and dormitory units, providing shops, cafeterias, and laundry facilities for its workers. Within the gates and fences of the city, the military attempted to provide every necessary service for its workers and residents. As one worker recalled, these incentives quickly became viewed as part of daily life. He recalled that "bus service was free— you just got on the bus. . . . They provided free coal, the electricity was free, the rent was practically nothing, they did it in order to entice people to Oak Ridge."[5]

The recruitment pitches made to draw workers and their families to the city were not forgotten by workers after they arrived; they were viewed by workers as promises, and the army and the companies were expected to deliver. When housing did not live up to expectations, when food and laundry services were found wanting, and when the pay was eroded by wartime inflation, a sense of grievance grew among residents of the city. Though wartime security and the rush to produce the bomb kept these issues quiet for the duration of the war, the end of conflict would bring these issues to the surface. Rather than privileges to be bestowed by a paternalistic government or employer, workers would argue that these were rights that had been earned by patriotic service.

The War Manpower Commission Searches for Workers

The WMC, charged with regulating and coordinating the flow of workers in war industries, realized early on that the Manhattan Project had a seemingly unlimited demand for workers. A December 1943 WMC report for Knoxville, Tennessee, noted that "the unknown demand at Clinton Engineer Works overshadows all known demand. Despite hiring, which has taken place at this project for the past four months, it is entirely possible that the demand for the forecast period will double or triple the known demand." Although the WMC cooperated in recruitment, labor shortages were chronic at Oak Ridge. In 1943, the project estimated that it would need 11,117 recruits to bring its labor force up to necessary staffing levels. This number included 1,851 carpenters, 530 electricians, and 4,482 laborers and tenders. Two years later, the project speculated that it needed 4,000 more workers to staff the factories at Oak Ridge, over and above those required to replace workers that quit or were fired from the project. Lack of sufficient manpower could have delayed the project as much as any scientific or technological setback, and Groves personally kept track of manpower and labor problems.[6]

Though the Manhattan Project is often portrayed as suffering from a shortage of physicists and other scientists, the truth is different. The project actually had a surplus of scientists and a shortage of electricians and plumbers. The wartime office diary of General Groves details numerous production bottlenecks caused by vast needs for scarce construction laborers. Skilled construction labor in particular was in short supply. Groves noted on June 19, 1944, "[Oak Ridge construction contractor] J. A. Jones needs 300–400 electricians" and suggested "securing loans of electricians through unions for a period of from 4 to 6 months." The delays that could be caused by lack of men to wire up new factories or connect the pipes used for manufacturing processes threatened to bring the project to a halt. One month later, Groves wrote, "One of the areas completely down for lack of pipefitters. . . . [They] have reached the point where they are talking of delay of a month."[7]

The nearby city of Knoxville could spare only a trickle of marginal surplus workers for work at Oak Ridge. The WMC estimated that in 1943–44, there would be only four hundred unemployed men and one thousand new female entrants in the labor market to draw upon. With such a "seller's market," and the additional security limitations imposed upon a recruiter's ability to describe the job or area, the army offered potential recruits higher-than-average wages and on-site housing, among other enticements. As one recruiter put it, "We gave them more money, we gave them a free bus ride, and we gave them rooms for $2 and a half." However, this strategy did not guarantee success in drawing enough workers to the site.[8]

The secrecy surrounding the work at Oak Ridge made recruiting even more difficult. One advertisement for common labor at the project provided few details to interest workers: "Construction laborers needed by vital war job in the vicinity of Knoxville, Tennessee. Working 58 hours per week—$0.575 per hour for 40 hours, plus $0.8625 per hour for additional 18 hours, making a weekly total of $38, weather permitting. Adequate facilities for room and board on project reservation. Transportation paid. . . . Apply United States Employment Service of the War Manpower Commission."[9] Such tepid help wanted ads retarded the recruitment effort. Without a description of the location of the work, or an inkling of the product of the facility, workers could not be expected to sign on in droves. The advertisement above served as an accurate preview of work and life in the facility, however, workers would learn the purpose of their labor only after the end of the war.

Faced with a labor shortage in Knoxville, many Oak Ridge contractors scoured the hinterlands for workers. The Tennessee Eastman Corporation (TEC) recruited in Knoxville, Lenoir City, and La Follette and surveyed households to determine potential employees. Stone and Webster Engineering, a construction contractor, recruited throughout the rural South, stopping in one recruiting tour at Tutwiler, Marks, Webb, Batesville, Sardis, and Crenshaw, Mississippi. In one Tennessee city, a manufacturer of ferromanganese complained that Stone and Webster, to circumvent wartime restriction of employed workers' movements, was "encouraging our men to quit and take 30 days off to qualify them to take a job at [Oak Ridge]. We have recently lost a large number of employees on this account and unless it is stopped promptly we will be forced to curtail production."[10] As one war industry poached employees from another, the WMC was drawn into the case, though it declined to punish Stone and Webster.

Recruitment became a covert operation for companies in need of construction labor. J. A. Jones Construction sent recruiters into rural Georgia, Arkansas, Mississippi, and Alabama in search of workers and trucked them north without receiving clearance from the WMC. Farmers and other employers in these areas filed complaints with the WMC against the company for illegal recruiting, particularly in Mississippi and Alabama. In August 1943, WMC officials in Alabama complained that "a Jones construction representative [backed up] a truck on the parking lot at the United States Employment Service office in Mobile, and presumed to load it up with some forty Negroes to be transported to a construction job in Knoxville." The Alabama WMC charged Jones with "labor pirating," though no penalty was imposed for this incident.[11]

The army combed the South for workers at Oak Ridge. In 1944, the MED sent forty-one recruiters out across the region in search of workers, targeting Nashville, Memphis, Knoxville, and Chattanooga in Tennessee, as well as cities in Virginia, Georgia, and Alabama. Skilled construction workers, such as carpenters, electricians, and plumbers, were drawn from as far away as New York City and Philadelphia, through skilled trades unions.[12]

Recruitment, however, was only the first step in getting a worker into the factories. Workers then needed to pass through employment and security screenings. According to an unpublished diary by T. E. Lane, an official with the Carbide and Carbon Chemical Corporation, an Oak Ridge Contractor, his company recruited "about 400 candidates per week, and half of these were screened out in the preliminary interview." Moreover, primitive living conditions led qualified applicants to refuse jobs. Lane noted that "security requirements were high, and those who could meet the high security requirements, would not live in the housing available." Once located and accepted, employees then had to be trained, and between one thousand and twelve hundred workers were in training at any one time for Carbide and Carbon alone. Just as scientists and engineers struggled to produce grams of usable material out of tons of unprocessed uranium ore, personnel recruiters and trainers such as Lane struggled to build a workforce and community out of the limited raw materials of homefront America.[13]

Recruiters located thousands of workers for the facility. However, job training, security requirements, and other barriers meant that only a fraction of those recruited ever made it into the workplace. At Tennessee Eastman, young female recruiters were sent to Arkansas, North Carolina, and Kentucky in search of women who were graduating high school and looking for work. Each year of the war, recruiters interviewed fifteen to twenty thousand potential female employees, yielding only seventeen hundred TEC workers. Men at Tennessee Eastman were recruited by advertisements and word of mouth, yielding as many as one thousand applicants per day—but few of these ended up in the plants. A combination of factors led to the low number of workers per applicant: security, job requirements, and, most important, whether workers were willing to sign on to work at Oak Ridge at the end of the interview and clearance process.[14]

Who Was Recruited?

The U.S. Army and its contractors recruited their workforce from a few key groups: coal miners, farmers, and men and women involved in rural industry. Each of these groups had seen hard times in the 1930s, and they were attracted to the relatively high cash wages paid at Oak Ridge. Former coal miners provided a large group of workers for Oak Ridge, because of the location of the facility in a coal mining area. During World War II, Tennessee ranked tenth in the nation in coal production; in Anderson county, 20 percent of men over age fourteen worked in the mines. In her autobiographical novel *The War at Home,* Connie Green describes her family's journey from coal country, where her father was a mine supervisor, to Oak Ridge, where he worked in one of the plants. The atmosphere of Oak Ridge, the company-owned housing, and the long hours resembled life in coal towns. The most striking difference was that in Oak Ridge, workers' children attended school until age eighteen, instead of leaving at fourteen to work in the mines. For many parents, including Green's, a chance at a high school education was the determining factor in relocating to Oak Ridge.[15]

Farmers served as another source of Oak Ridge's workers. Some worked on a seasonal basis, returning to their home community in the summer after a winter of construction at Oak Ridge, while others commuted to Oak Ridge every week. These workers boarded with farm families surrounding the complex before returning to their farms on weekends. John Corbin VanHooser and his brother-in-law Shelah Daniel, for example, were concrete construction workers who commuted weekly from their farms near Woodbury, Tennessee, some 130 miles southwest of Oak Ridge. These workers stayed first with the family of a miner at Coalmont and later with a farm family outside Lenoir City. Others used the money gained at Oak Ridge to support their farm, which they rented to sharecroppers or left to the management of wives and families in their absence. Finally, there were farmers who aspired to be landowners and sought money through industrial work to pay for their start in agriculture. Manhattan Project officials understood that their project was not the top priority for workers, noting that they had to recruit "even farmers in the vicinity who found it necessary to absent themselves frequently in order to keep their farms going."[16]

Other workers migrated from industrial facilities, rural or urban. Typical of these workers was Oliver Evans, a production worker originally from Metropolis, Illinois, who served two and a half years in the Pacific with the army then came to Oak Ridge to work in the plants, drawn by high wages. He, like many others, remained after the end of the war. Others workers came from southern industries such as lumber processing. Oak Ridge workers from Mississippi told WMC interviewers that the offer of a higher paying job category brought them to Knoxville. James Anderson of Philadelphia, Mississippi, told the WMC, "I quit working for the lumber company because I was not making enough money to support my family. I made between $20–25 per week." Jessie Red Collins reported, "I quit the lumber company as I asked for a raise, and they wouldn't give it to me. [The recruiter] told me that he would give me 67.5 cents per hour to come to Tennessee to work on a government project." Harvey Hartfield of Carthage, Mississippi, explained, "I quit for more money. [The recruiter] told me a government job opened up here at Knoxville and would pay me 67.5 cents/hour and I could get as many hours as I wanted 7 days/week."[17] The low wages of southern rural industry propelled many workers to Oak Ridge, as pay and working conditions there could only get better.

Many workers came to Oak Ridge with their entire family, as the facility could provide jobs for both males and females. Colleen Black remembered:

> We moved from a two story house in Nashville to a double trailer in K-25 [a mobile home camp for construction workers] . . . , my mother and father and eight brothers and sisters. I was the ninth child. The tenth child was fighting in the army overseas. That's why we came to Oak Ridge— to win the war, to bring him home. . . . My mother had never worked before, but she went down and got a job. My father worked at J. A. Jones, and I worked at [Oak Ridge construction contractor] Ford, Bacon and Davis, and mother worked at Carbide.

For Black, Oak Ridge was a step up for the entire family, as jobs were available for all family members above the age of eighteen.[18]

Owing to the draft, Oak Ridge workers ranged from slightly older than average (for men) to generally young (for women). Tennessee Eastman Corporation hired workers at an average age of twenty-eight for women and thirty-five for men. Fewer than one-half of Y-12 workers were high school graduates, though 67 percent had graduated from at least eighth grade. Even in 1949, when Carbide and Carbon published a survey of its workers, more than half of its male workers were below age thirty-six, and half of its female workers were twenty-eight or younger. Since little new hiring had occurred between 1945 and 1948, it can be estimated that the average Oak Ridge worker at the end of the war was between twenty-four and thirty-two years old.[19]

Arriving in Oak Ridge
NO ROOM AT THE INN

The first feeling many workers had upon reaching the facility was power-lessness over their daily lives. One worker recalled entry to Oak Ridge as a series of inconveniences caused by poor planning and overcrowded facil-ities. The house he had been promised when recruited did not yet exist, and no housing was available in the city of Oak Ridge. This sent him to Knoxville in search of a hotel, but the hotel had no rooms save a common bedroom filled with cots where war workers slept around the clock, depend-ing on their shift. He remembered, "I did not sleep a wink that night—people came in and out all night." Soon he was shifted to a house, shared by many workmen, and finally to a dormitory, where he spent his first months at the facility, before sending for his wife to join him. These expe-riences let workers know, early in their Oak Ridge experiences, that life would be very different here.[20]

The federal government's control of housing, through its contractor, Roane-Anderson, also rankled workers. Many families resented being assigned to cramped trailers. In the dormitories, where privacy was limited, Roane-Anderson employees kept track of rules against drinking, gambling, and visitors of the opposite sex. Worse, the company tracked employment of their lodgers; those who lost their job in Oak Ridge were liable for imme-diate eviction. This heavy-handed system was designed to maintain Oak Ridge's reputation as a safe place to live, as well as to assign housing to those most in need. However, by zealously enforcing these rules, the company made the city's residents only more desperate to make their way out of the dormi-tories into houses and apartments where they would be left alone.

Workers arriving at Oak Ridge faced an unequal housing system. At the bottom of the hierarchy were African Americans, housed by the army in a fenced-in neighborhood of hutments. For whites, housing was assigned according to job and rank. The shortage of housing caused by massive recruiting and construction delays only made the situation worse. Houses, the most sought-after form of living quarters, were restricted by the army to "heads of household" (men) earning more than sixty dollars a week in salary. Hourly workers, no matter how highly paid or necessary to the suc-cess of the project, had no chance of winning this coveted commodity.

Local residents who lived within forty miles also were denied the chance at an Oak Ridge house. For hourly workers, trailers, hutments, dormitories, and apartments were the only housing available. These small quarters did not guarantee privacy, as accommodations were shared by several unrelated individuals because of housing shortages. While managers, engineers, and scientists resided on scenic Outer Drive, the vast majority of Oak Ridgers lived in the cramped quarters of trailers, dorms, and hutments that formed the valley below.[21]

The first experiences of the security system also help to show new workers and residents where they stood. One worker remembered, "Even after you got in the gate, you weren't free to go. When we were interviewed to be employed, I remembered that there was just a small area where we could go, and then we had to go back out, . . . and they were always checking your pass and being sure that you were supposed to be where you were." Workers were scheduled around the clock, making normal family life difficult during the war. One worker recalled that the sleep schedule of her mother, father, and siblings "had to rotate, because there were only four beds in the double trailer. . . . Of course, every house and every trailer had blackout curtains, because people were sleeping around the clock." The combination of cramped accommodations and schedules made life in Oak Ridge different from family life back home for most workers, as did the higher rates of employment for women in the city.[22]

Broken Promises I
WOMEN

At Oak Ridge, as in other parts of the country during World War II, women moved into industrial work in unprecedented numbers. As photographs from Oak Ridge during the war demonstrate (fig. 2), women formed a significant proportion of the workforce, particularly at Y-12. However, unlike the situation in other war industries, women at Oak Ridge did not replace men in the factories but were present in the formative stages of the industry. Oak Ridge companies recruited rural women from the region for both office and factory jobs. For women from rural backgrounds, these jobs were a significant step up the economic ladder. Helen Hall, just out of high school in 1943, took a job at Tennessee Eastman in Oak Ridge because it offered "higher pay than any factories paid in the area" and she saw it as a way of "helping the boys" in the war. For women, working at Oak Ridge was attractive compared to other low-wage jobs available to them elsewhere in the South, such as the textile industry. In addition, the organized social activ-

This shift change at Y-12 reveals the role of women in
keeping Y-12 up and running, c. 1944. Box 23, Binder 69,
RG 434-OR, Still Pictures Branch, NARA.

ities at the facility, such as weekly dances and movies, gave women more
freedom than normally was possible in most rural, coal, or textile town set-
tings. Many of these women remained in Oak Ridge after the war, taking
permanent jobs or marrying men who worked there.

Women whose husbands were unemployed or not in the area worked
at Oak Ridge to support their families. Lillie Phillips was a professional
housekeeper at Oak Ridge, cleaning dormitory rooms. In addition to her
paid labor, she kept house at her own home for as many as eleven relatives,
who passed through Oak Ridge to work or to travel to other employment.
Phillips, the sole wage earner, depended on her job to keep herself and her
children economically afloat.[23]

Other women worked keeping house and finding food and supplies for
male and female relatives who worked at the plants. As one woman told an
interviewer about her mother, "It was a full-time job to find food to put
on her table." Oak Ridge residents faced long lines for food, laundry, and
other day-to-day necessities, adding hours to women's workweek. For

women who worked in the plants, the pressures to be at work and to run a home were almost intolerable. Even though Oak Ridge provided a laundry service for workers and their families, and housekeeping services were provided in dormitories, shopping was a full-time job in itself. "An Employed Couple" complained to the *Oak Ridge Journal:* "If we are on the job from 7 am to 5 pm, as we are requested and urged, when we drive to the trailer camp— all the stores are ready to close. Everything has been picked over until only the worse and sometimes none is left. . . . If this project's main aim is winning the war, THEN WHY NOT GIVE WORKING COUPLES A CHANCE SO THAT THEY CAN BE ON THE JOB AND HELP GET THIS THING OVER WITH?"[24]

Lack of housing and child care hit women hardest, especially those who were the sole wage earners. Oak Ridge housing policy was sex-biased, viewing women as dependents who were not eligible to register for a place to live. Mona Myers, a TEC production worker, wrote to the WMC:

> I do know that you have asked us women who could to go to work. I am taking training for a war job at Tennessee Eastman. While in training a representative of our company signed us up for a house. Now that I am in the area they tell me that because my husband does not work for our company I am not eligible for a house, even though I make enough to look after my family. . . . My husband is a Southern Railway employee and only home during the weekends, so I have to be home part of each day because I have two small daughters. . . . I don't understand why if we women can do a man's job we can't rent a house. . . . If industry is going to do this to women, how can they ask us to leave our homes and families and go to work?[25]

Women played a vital role in Oak Ridge's labor force. However, in the factories at Oak Ridge, women workers were segregated into low-status, lower-paying jobs where they tended or monitored production machinery. Women's grievances within the factories and in the community were, in many ways, greater than those held by men. However, sex segregation kept women apart from other Oak Ridge workers. The companies, as well as the women themselves, were aware that these wartime jobs for women were considered "temporary," until the plants closed or the men returned from war.

Broken Promises II
AFRICAN AMERICANS

World War II offered unparalleled economic opportunities for African American workers. Whole industries once closed to African Americans openly recruited their labor. Under pressure from African American leaders, most notably union leader A. Phillip Randolph, the federal government set up the Fair Employment Practices Committee (FEPC) to curb racial discrimination in war industries. For the first time since Reconstruction, the federal government sought some measure of economic justice for African American workers. However, many federal policies lacked legal teeth and strong enforcement. While the FEPC held hearings and made findings of racial discrimination, the War Department did nothing to bar discriminatory contractors from war work. As Andrew Kersten demonstrates in his recent book *Race, Jobs and the War*, the agency was ineffective even in major manufacturing areas and centers of African American activism such as Detroit and Chicago, where media attention cast the light on discriminatory practices. In the Oak Ridge area, with security preventing media scrutiny, and with a small and rural African American population, the FEPC had little impact.[26]

Despite national policies aimed at reducing racial discrimination, the federal government imposed a system of racial segregation at Oak Ridge. The area in which Oak Ridge was located had been a checkerboard of black and white farms and communities for generations, but when the army built the city of Oak Ridge, it created separate "Colored" and "White" living areas. The army segregated housing, shopping, and transportation in the city. Through leases and contracts, the army controlled the businesses and the bus system at Oak Ridge and used this power to enforce racial segregation. One white resident remembers that as a small child, a bus driver chased him to the front of the bus because he was sitting in the "wrong section." The army constructed segregated and unequal communities for black and white workers at Oak Ridge. At the beginning of the war, black married couples were forced to live apart: black women lived in segregated dormitories while black men lived in the "colored hutments"—one small room, without plumbing, rented to four men or women at a time. As contemporary photographs show, these hutments were a solid step down from other forms of Oak Ridge housing, such as dormitories or trailers (fig. 3).[27]

The Manhattan Project did not invent the practice of racial segregation in company towns. It drew from the experience of coal companies, which, if they hired blacks at all, housed them in separate sections of the company town. Additionally, the project's segregation was modeled after Tennessee Valley Authority policy, which had housed black workers in separate and substandard housing at dam construction sites in Tennessee. Oak Ridge contractors, like Tennessee Eastman, operated in planned segregated communities such as Kingsport, Tennessee. Segregation extended even to recreation halls and cafeterias—with inferior facilities assigned to

Hutments such as this one served as housing for Oak Ridge's
African American community throughout the 1940s. Box 8,
Binder 24, RG 434-OR, Still Pictures Branch, NARA.

African Americans. As MED photographs show, the food and entertain-
ment facilities available to the African American community were ill-
furnished and poorly maintained, not up to the standards of the rest of
Oak Ridge. The practice of federally sponsored segregation had its roots
in the 1930s. As Arnold Hirsch and Gail Radford have demonstrated, federal building projects in the 1930s and 1940s concentrated African
Americans into small areas, increasing the level of segregation in urban
areas. The situation at Oak Ridge was a micro-version of the trend that
shaped urban centers such as Chicago. Rapid urbanization and industri-
alization of the Anderson and Roane county areas led to the creation of a
segregated African American community inside Oak Ridge, where no such
concentration had existed before.[28]

The army and companies defended the practice of racial segregation as an adaptation to the racial mores of the area. One personnel officer recalled that the "government had to attract people to the project with houses near to what they were used to. Black housing was better than what a black worker in Mississippi would have had, while a white scientist wouldn't feel the same way." However, both the conditions of the hutments and the top-down imposition of racial segregation horrified many whites. One worker recalled that the "black hutments [were] a real disgrace." Though whites did little (and could do little) during the war to change army policies, this obvious discrimination led some white Oak Ridgers to work for school and housing desegregation in the 1950s. However, this response was by no means universal. Pictures of Oak Ridge shops during World War II feature Whites Only signs that are unmistakable evidence that not all white Oak Ridgers wished to share social space with blacks.[29]

After arriving at Oak Ridge by bus or truck, African Americans confronted many of the same problems they hoped they had left behind in the Deep South. They were disappointed to learn that previously undisclosed racial policies limited their earning power. African American worker Lee Crawford told the WMC, "I quit working for the S. K. Fergusen company because [the recruiter] told me that I could make 7–8 cents more per hour in Tennessee as a truck driver or tractor operator. Upon arriving here I was told colored people were not allowed to drive trucks." African Americans were assigned the most menial and unskilled tasks— as common laborers, janitors, and domestic workers. The few photographs that exist of African American workers during the war show that they were consigned to the bottom of the employment ladder, and that many of jobs were worked exclusively by African Americans (fig. 4). Blacks were ineligible for transfers to higher paying job categories or for promotion by the companies at Oak Ridge and were often discriminated against for skilled construction or production jobs.[30]

Why did African Americans come to Oak Ridge, to endure segregation and work at the lowest-paying jobs? Oak Ridge resident and writer Valerie Steele explains that blacks received "higher pay than they had ever known." For many, "the Great Depression years had been . . . harsh and forbidding. Life had been a sheer struggle for survival, living on the bare edge of existence. In Oak Ridge, some of these conditions were alleviated, if not eliminated." As one African American resident told Steele, "Everybody was so glad to have a job making some money. We weren't making money back home." In spite of racial discrimination, work at Oak Ridge generally paid much better than work elsewhere in the South. Construction laborers made a minimum of 57.5 cents per hour, plus overtime, for a weekly total averaging $38. Since this was a 50 percent raise for some workers, it was a significant draw northward. In the midst of a South that still clung to sharecropping and domestic service as the major job opportunities for blacks, a high cash wage was a key to greater personal freedom as well as prosperity.[31]

African Americans were restricted to low-skill jobs in
Oak Ridge, c. 1945. Box 4, Notebook 14, RG 434-OR,
Still Pictures Branch, NARA.

Promises Kept and Broken

The recruitment strategy of the Manhattan Project made an impact on Oak Ridge's later history in ways the army did not predict. Oak Ridge recruited most of its workers through nonwage incentives and promises that made industrial work at Oak Ridge more appealing than existing farm or factory work. Workers viewed these promises as a reward for their term of duty as industrial soldiers. In the postwar years, workers viewed these recruitment strategies as unkept promises, which in turn encouraged labor organizing around the issues of housing, steadiness of work, and wages. When, at the end of the war, the army sought to raise rents, lay off workers, and trim social programs, workers viewed these actions as breaking the contract that had attracted them to Oak Ridge. The recruitment strategy of the Manhattan Project sowed the seeds of future worker discontent.

CHAPTER 3

Who Controls the Job Site?
Construction and Skilled Trades Workers

IN OAK RIDGE and across the United States, World War II was a time of "divided consciousness" for American workers. On the one hand, working for a war industry took on the tenor of patriotic duty. Not only did workers contribute to the war effort through their welding, riveting, and assembling, but they also bought war bonds and contributed directly from their pay envelope to donate money for war materiel. However, this sense of patriotic duty did not mean that workers were willing to abandon all rights on the job. They did not wish to give up the economic gains they made in the 1930s as a result of union organizing, and they resisted heavy-handed management. Contrary to popular portrayals of World War II as a time of social consensus on the homefront, the years 1942 to 1945 were a high point in American labor conflict. Across the nation, workers walked out of their jobs over issues of pay, shop-floor control, long hours, and poor working conditions.[1]

Construction and skilled trade workers in Oak Ridge were viewed as both workers and industrial soldiers. While New Deal labor policy had given workers a legal right to strike, the beginning of the war and the "no strike pledge" between unions and the federal government limited union actions. Nevertheless, workers did not completely buy into the definition of industrial soldiers with its rights and obligations; like the public culture of patriotism developed by the government, workers constructed a patriotic rhetoric to advance their cause on the job. In Oak Ridge, construction and skilled trades workers protested when pushed too hard to increase production. Through absenteeism, wildcat strikes, and other job actions, workers pressed their grievances against management or the federal government, often framing their demands in terms of patriotism and their rights as citizens, rather than with the language of their rights as workers.

Unions in Oak Ridge
A DIVIDED WORKFORCE

In 1944, General Groves faced a dilemma in formulating a labor policy for the Manhattan Project. Although the project sought to forestall union organization in Oak Ridge's plants, labor shortages on the homefront meant that the army needed to use labor unions to recruit skilled workers. In addition, Groves wanted to maximize the efficiency of workers, but in a tight labor market it was difficult to discipline or fire workers who could simply move on to another high-paying war job. Part of Groves's attitude toward labor is evident in his siting of Oak Ridge. He looked for a site in "friendly," non-union territory, according to one biographer. In locating the Oak Ridge facility, Groves had to contend only with local Knoxville American Federation of Labor (AFL) unions, rather than the powerful Congress of Industrial Organizations (CIO) unions found in the Northeast and Midwest.[2]

General Groves viewed himself as the commanding officer of the Manhattan Project's workers, a profoundly autocratic view of labor relations. He sought to channel and control labor much as he sought to buy and direct the flow of raw materials. For Groves, the complex system of the Manhattan Project required a strong central manager (himself) who could send orders directly from Washington to the construction site at Oak Ridge. David Noble describes Groves's management style perfectly: "The military term for management is command, a rather straightforward notion that means the superior gives the orders and the subordinate executes them, no ifs, ands, or buts." However, Groves could not simply impose his command on Oak Ridge's workers, because if enough of them quit their jobs, the project was finished. War Department attorney John Ohly was assigned to help Groves craft a labor policy that would attract and retain workers at Oak Ridge while giving Groves the command he desired. Ohly, in order to forestall union organizing and keep turnover rates low, sought to keep workers content with their wages and working and living conditions.[3]

Initially, Groves did not believe that labor unions should be allowed in Oak Ridge. In November 1944, he described the goals of his labor policy at Oak Ridge in terms of production expediency and security. The most important of these goals were "getting out the production required in accordance with schedules, ... safeguarding the operation from sabotage or other subversive interference, and preventing the disclosure of any information [that] ... might benefit a foreign power [and] ... obtaining the highest degree of efficiency and economy of operations." Unions, Groves wrote, would make these goals impossible to meet. He noted that "if unions are permitted to exist on the project, a whole series of difficult problems arise which could be avoided if unions were not present." Problems included breaches of security, jurisdictional disputes, strikes, union control of hiring, "organizational activity which may be disruptive to production," and the flow of information to international union officers.[4]

However, Groves's most important objection was that unions would lead to security problems. He wrote, "If unions are permitted, there will be union meetings which will be a hazard to security. . . . Union meetings are more dangerous because they may bring together people engaged in related work and who are likely to talk about their work." These meetings would need to be "controlled in the same fashion as the meetings of all other organizations on the project." Therefore, because of production and security concerns, he suggested barring union organizing at Oak Ridge for the duration of the war.[5]

Ohly disagreed. He noted that workers possess "the right to join a union" under the Wagner Act and that "this is a clearly established right to which there are no exceptions." He argued that this right to organize would be enforced by workers themselves, as it "is the most zealously guarded right of organized labor, in fact its foundation stone, and the War Department would be unrealistic to attempt openly or secretly to abrogate it." He continued, "There is no practical way, short of discharge or exclusion from the project, in which the War Department can prevent men joining, or organizing themselves into unions, if they really wish to do so." Firing union members or driving them off the project grounds would be dangerous because "the only effect . . . would be to drive any union underground or force it to carry on its meetings off the project. . . . From a security standpoint it would be far more difficult to control in any fashion." He did not believe it would be necessary to exclude unions from the project if "living and working conditions on the project, and wage rates, are such that there may be a lack of incentives for workers to band together." He recommended that "continuance of the best possible conditions, including the application of the fairest possible grievance procedures, . . . would make the general development of unions unlikely."[6]

Groves decided to recognize and negotiate with AFL construction unions, as he needed them to recruit skilled workers. However, production workers who manned the factories at Oak Ridge would be prevented from organizing unions. Thus, unions would be free to operate in the construction site, but their influence would stop at the factory gates. Groves justified this decision on two grounds. He assumed that "95 percent of construction workers never come in contact with classified information or materials, whereas the converse is true with production workers." More important, however, was the fact that "the construction workers who came to the project . . . were already union members organized into strong unions, and the unions were themselves instrumental in staffing the . . . project."[7]

Therefore, the War Department requested that the National Labor Relations Board postpone action on any worker's request for official union recognition. At the same time, Groves asked top AFL, CIO, and United Mine Workers officials to keep local unions from organizing in the plants at Oak Ridge. On November 29, 1944, Groves learned that his request to postpone NLRB action on unions at Oak Ridge had been granted. The NLRB would not process worker petitions for the duration of the war. In December 1944, he learned that District 50, the United Mine Workers' organization for industrial workers, "had tried to get in the area but without success and as far as we can ascertain there hasn't been any [District 50 activity] on the project at all." Thus, the labor policy adopted by Groves included postponement of union organizing in the production plants, a policy to which national union leaders and the NLRB acquiesced.[8]

Skilled Construction Workers
JOB CONTROL AT THE SITE

Though the U.S. Army sought a workforce that would work quickly and efficiently to produce a maximum of atomic materials at a minimum of cost, skilled construction exerted more control over their work than did their production counterparts. This control was based on a number of factors, such as high demand for skilled labor and the nature of the work done by those in skilled trades. Since these trades worked outside, in groups, and set their own work pace, they were far more difficult to control than production workers. Conflicts over job control between contractors and the construction trades were a common occurrence on the Manhattan Project, whether they took the form of passive resistance to managerial policies (such as absenteeism) or wildcat walkouts.

The first right construction workers on the project regularly exercised was the right to not appear for work. Absenteeism and labor turnover plagued the management of the Manhattan Project, among both skilled and unskilled workers. The army recognized that failure to appear for work was often a silent protest against management policies, caused by worker dissatisfaction with their jobs and Oak Ridge living conditions. These chronic shortages prompted Groves to consider using prisoners, Italian prisoners of war, and Mexican braceros as labor for the project, ultimately rejecting these options owing to problems of housing these groups separately.[9]

The army developed a "presenteeism" campaign in which companies and their workers won recognition for the highest percentage of men present each day on the job. This campaign encouraged workers not to take time off and labeled those with poor attendance records as unpatriotic. The army suggested to one construction company that another contractor had good results when "men are terminated who habitually absent themselves during the week but report for work on premium days," and when weekly War Bond raffles were held, only those with good attendance records were eligible. The William Pope Company, stressing that workers were soldiers on the homefront, hung signs that pictured a time clock and stated, "This is your bazooka! Don't fail to use it! Stay on the job!" Signage throughout Oak Ridge stressed the need to appear on the job in order to support troops in the field and defeat the enemy quickly (fig. 5).[10]

The second right construction trades fought to maintain was control over the work process on the job site. Once specifications had been set and timetables solidified, trades resented managerial interference with their work, particularly attempts to wring more work out of them. During the war, the army and company managers defined efficiency in terms of their own command over the workforce; the wartime ideology of workers as industrial soldiers gave them an excuse to restructure the workplace to maximum production. Wartime propaganda stressed the need for greater production and, by implication, made questioning production strategies look unpatriotic. However, these production drives at Oak Ridge were resisted, particularly by skilled craft workers who sought to retain control of their work pace. In fact, the struggle over efficiency and control reveals that skilled workers outside the plants had a great deal of control over their work. However, with a shortage of skilled labor and vast work sites to monitor, the skilled workers who built Oak Ridge enjoyed far more freedom to set the pace of their own work than any production workers.

Manhattan Engineer District leaders and contractors designed and implemented an "efficiency campaign" to change work practices at Oak Ridge, attempting to give management more control over the skilled workforce. Though workers were asked to give their input into the campaign, it was the contractors and the army who ran the campaign with their own purposes in mind. The results of this campaign demonstrate that workers and managers had completely different meanings of the term "efficiency." Workers submitted ideas to the campaign that stressed positive reinforcement

Propaganda posters give a strong sense of the range of patriotic
messages given to workers in Oak Ridge, c. 1944. Box 4,
Notebook 12, RG 434-OR, Still Pictures Branch, NARA.

and encouraged the army bureaucracy to be more responsive to workers'
needs. Sven Ekhalm, a cable splicer on the project, thought that "service rib-
bons" for three or six months of uninterrupted war work would help boost
morale and serve to shame "slackers" into better attendance. Workers at the
A S. Schulman Electric Company wrote that "improvement of food in the
cafeterias" and "simplifying the procedure for obtaining tires and gasoline
from the rationing board" would increase efficiency. For workers, efficiency
meant that the army's bureaucracy should work for them and support their
efforts on the job.[11]

Contractors defined efficiency primarily in terms of restructuring the
workplace to give management more control over the work process.
A. S. Schulman Electric, as part of its efficiency plan, told the men that
"idleness, loafing and unexcused absences will be reason for discharge for
cause." The Stone and Webster company reported that "supervisors and
foremen have been instructed to discharge loafers. An examination of ter-

mination records for the project shows that loafers and undesirables are being weeded out." The director of Clinton Laboratories told the District Engineer's office of their "intent to dispense with the services of inefficient personnel." In 1944, recruiting efforts were increased in an attempt to have more employees to replace those fired for laziness.[12]

The Schulman company instituted a policy of "spot checks . . . to insure maximum efficiency and organizational balance" and instructed foremen to "weed out inefficient personnel who will not respond to instructions and will not put forth an effort to turn out a reasonable days work." A company letter to employees let them know that "avoidable absenteeism is sabotage at its worst" and that "loafing, inefficiency and time-killing will be cause for dismissal. . . . An employee terminated for cause may not be reemployed at the Clinton Engineer Works." Every moment was of concern to the efficiency campaigners. As part of the campaign, J. A. Jones Construction shortened cafeteria hours in the morning to prevent eating on the job and checked to make sure that employees ate their lunch quickly. This issue found its way into Oak Ridge propaganda signs, in which loafing was defined as unpatriotic and a crime against ones own family (fig. 6).[13]

H. V. Appen, a project manager for J. A. Jones, described some of the barriers to maximum efficiency: "There is entirely too much loafing on the job. . . . Very few men actually start on time. . . . Their main thought seems to be to punch the time clock before the whistle blows. We must remind them that the whistle blowing means for the men to start work and not rushing through the clock aisles. . . . Men are quitting ahead of time, in order to get a front seat next to the clock aisles at punching out time. . . . Believe it or not, every day we are finding men asleep on the job, on government time and government pay." Appen told his compressor operators that they "will refrain from lying down at and around their compressors, and will try to assume a vertical position as much as possible." Attempts to control work and work pace applied to lunch as well. Appen told his truck drivers to discontinue "giving rides to a great number of workmen before or at lunch time to the several cafeterias," as the men should instead bring their lunch with them in order to save time on the job. These rules, presumably created to address existing problems, illustrate that employees viewed their work time as a combination of labor and leisure time. They did not view their lining up early to clock in and out as privileges but as a rational reaction to the inconvenience and inefficiency of the work system at Oak Ridge.[14]

Since many workers were putting in ten- to twelve-hour days and six- to seven-day weeks, work was not viewed as a nonstop activity, as this would

Messages about "loafing" were aimed at getting workers to contribute
their maximum at all times, c. 1945. Box 20, Notebook 59,
RG 434-OR, Still Pictures Branch, NARA.

be physically impossible. The contest over efficiency between workers and
managers suggest that labor at many Oak Ridge work sites alternated
between hard work and rest, in which workers viewed themselves as on call
but felt little obligation to keep up constant activity (or the illusion thereof).
However, managers attempted to use the wartime emergency to justify their
increased power over skilled workers at job sites and to define efficiency as
uninterrupted labor. For the most part, this conflict was settled in terms
of low-level solutions—absenteeism, uneven enforcement of workplace
rules, and quitting work when conditions seemed better somewhere far-
ther north. However, in several instances, groups of construction workers
at Oak Ridge struck to protect their rights, in defiance of the army, their
managers, and their unions.

Examples of this view of labor, with workers on call when needed, come
from many of the crime and security reports filed in Oak Ridge. A manager reported that a welder was accused of harassing women at Y-12 after

midnight. Security officers found him, surrounded by beer bottles, sleeping in a shed outside the plant. He "admitted the beer was his and said that he didn't know there was any objection to beer on the job. He excused the sleeping on the grounds that he was on standby duty." Another security report, of a dice game at K-25, includes worker testimony that "all four claim they have standby jobs, and there was nothing for them to do at the moment, and their respective foremen and supervisors knew where to find them if needed." Though most employees were far more conscientious than those described above, workers throughout Oak Ridge viewed their workplace as a second home, to the point where one operated sales of bootleg whiskey from his crane.[15]

Breaking the Pledge
WARTIME STRIKES

Vincent Jones's *Manhattan: The Army and the Atomic Bomb* states, "Perhaps the most concrete evidence of the effectiveness of the project's labor policies was the almost complete absence of work stoppages from late 1944 to the end of the war. Manhattan Project production plants had lost only about 86 thousand man hours, or about 0.028 percent of their potential working time, as a result of work stoppages." However, this account leaves out the importance of those work conflicts that did escalate into walkouts.[16]

The pattern of the thirty-two walkouts at Oak Ridge demonstrate a great deal about the differences in construction and production work and skilled and unskilled work at the facility. Skilled construction workers struck far more often (thirty-one times) than those involved in production (one), and skilled trades within the construction field participated in more actions (twenty-five) than unskilled laborers (seven). Unions such as the Plumbers (six), Carpenters (five), and Electricians (four) struck the most, indicating that it was those in skilled crafts, especially those in highest demand, who felt able to walk out with confidence that they would not be fired for their action. Skilled workers were the backbone of resistance to managerial authority at Oak Ridge, and wages were not the primary issue of the majority of strikes. Complaints over wages and hours accounted for eight strikes (25 percent of actions), but conflicts over supervision and discipline were the leading cause of disputes, resulting in nine walkouts. Questions of jurisdiction and the closed shop caused seven disputes, and layoffs and working conditions led to four work actions each.[17]

With skilled workers in high demand and replacements hard to find, the Manhattan Project sometimes gave into worker demands, ignoring their own policy to fire strikers. For example, in August 1945, a group of machinists at Tennessee Eastman Corporation walked out over the issue of the proper start time and break times for their job. According to Manhattan Project records, "TEC machinists in building 9766 (Processing Laboratory) went out on strike this morning between 0900 and 0930. They gave as their reasons two grievances: 1. They are tired of waiting for a decision as to whether their hours are to be changed back from 08:15 to 17:00 to 07:15 to 15:45, and 2. They are of the opinion that they were allowed 15 minutes, morning and afternoon to clean up and change clothing, but they were docked yesterday for taking this usual period." The army promised to resolve the issue the next day, and workers agreed to return to the job, so long as they set the hours of work.[18]

Pipefitters and welders on the project were also in short supply and high demand, but they still went out of their way to ensure that their job actions did not appear unpatriotic. Working in an unventilated building in the heat of a Tennessee August, they walked off the job in protest over the lack of fans. The company had promised previously to install fans to ventilate the work site. On August 3, 1945, with no fans forthcoming, workers picked up their tools, clocked off the job, and went home, telling the company that they would not return until the fans were installed. Project labor relations officials ordered the contractor to install the fans that night, so that work could resume the next morning. With the fans installed, the pipefitters and welders agreed to return to work the next morning, and maintained that, in fact, there had never been a walkout at all, that the men had simply clocked out early to allow for installation of the fans. The men followed all of the rules of the company, down to clocking out before leaving, in order to demonstrate that they were not intentionally disrupting the project or the war effort.[19]

The army, however, viewed any sign of organization among Oak Ridge's guard force as a sign of disloyalty. In 1943, when two guards were discovered with applications for membership in the United Construction Workers (a United Mine Workers–affiliated union), the army circulated a list of those who were "probably supporters," identified the men involved, and discharged them.[20]

International Brotherhood of Electrical Workers (IBEW) craft workers objected to the dismissal of one of their members and demanded union recognition from their employer, Carbide and Carbon Chemical Corporation. The electricians who worked in the K-25 powerhouse had been told that as production workers, they could not organize for security reasons, but they would be recognized informally by the company and would have access to a grievance procedure for their complaints. The union found its requests for an officially recognized shop steward blocked by the company's argument that it would violate "security regulations." But a union official found this reasoning "absurd, since the manner in which power is produced is more or less standardized the world over" and "any janitor can glance up and see how much total load is produced," as the electrical meters were easily accessible.[21]

When electricians charged that company personnel were biased against union members, one was fired shortly thereafter. Fourteen men walked off the job, and all were fired as a result. Leslie Carr, a union electrician fired for his part in the walkout, wrote in protest, "The War Department requested the IBEW to postpone the [NLRB] hearing since the War Department believed the publicity of the court proceedings would jeopardize the security of the Clinton Engineer Workers [Oak Ridge]. The IBEW members at the plant, being good American citizens and 100 percent behind the war, instructed their representative to comply with the request of the War Department." The company, however, had "taken advantage of our patriotism, since we have postponed our legal rights in the matter because of patriotic reasons."[22]

This last example underscores the ways in which army policies restricted worker rights. Working at Oak Ridge meant that wages were high, work was steady, and housing, medical, educational, and social services were provided to workers and their families. Yet once the actions of workers crossed the line and could be seen as working against the war effort, or against what the army defined as patriotic, there was no recourse, as national unions and the NLRB had promised to stay out of Oak Ridge's problems. Loss of a job at Oak Ridge also meant being evicted from one's house in Oak Ridge and blacklisted from other Oak Ridge facilities, effectively losing one's citizenship rights in the community along with one's job.

Undisclosed Risks
SAFETY AND HEALTH ON THE JOB SITE

Security regulations prevented workers from learning about possible exposure to health hazards until after the war was over. As information was released to the public over the postwar period, many workers realized that they had been exposed to potential health hazards. One Oak Ridge skilled trades worker recalled:

> I got a call to bring some electricians to a secret warehouse on the east end of Oak Ridge, to put some fans in. The warehouses were getting so

hot that they were afraid that they were going to blow up. They told me, "You can take your men in there for 30 minutes, take them out for 40 minutes, then they can go back for another 30 minutes. I was curious about this, and when I went in, I saw all these sacks of what looked like fertilizer, about the width of a boxcar, five-foot high and maybe 80-foot length. . . . When the bomb was dropped, there was a picture in a newspaper of all these bags of uranium sitting on a dock in Canada. And that's when I realized what I had been looking at. And they didn't know at the time how much radiation you could get out of that.

Construction workers were routinely placed in situations in which exposure to radiation or other hazardous substances was possible. However, they were never given a choice to refuse a hazardous assignment, or told their exposure level. Instead, as in the case above, workers learned about the hazards of their work only retroactively, if at all.[23]

After the war, other construction workers complained of poor health after working at Oak Ridge. S. J. Matson, who worked there during the war, noted, "There are other electricians injured also from their association with that building we tore down, [and] like myself they were . . . informed they had nothing to fear as long as they followed safety rules." These rules did nothing at the site, where "material was wet down at the building to prevent the workmen from breathing radioactivated dust [but] it was not wet on in the field where we dumped the material to be buried under a scorching hot sun and the wind blowing." Mattson claimed that the burial ground was then labeled "Danger-Radioactivity."[24]

Construction and maintenance workers also faced serious hazards that were never addressed in the workplace. A TEC safety engineer, in a memo about poisonous gases in the workplace, noted, "The exposure of maintenance men is especially severe, since these men are not chemists by schooling, but skilled tradesmen employed in such capacities as electricians, pipefitters, etc. These persons are, in general, unlikely to consider a chemical risk a severe one since the hazard is one which cannot be seen but must, in general, be taken on trust." He noted that several skilled trades employees at TEC had endured "six gas exposures during the past year." The cases this engineer knew about were incomplete because no records were kept unless workers reported feeling ill.

It is impossible to reconstruct the hazards these men may have faced. Unlike production and operations workers, skilled trades workers rotated around plant areas at Oak Ridge, making it more difficult to track the source of their injuries. As a result, construction and skilled trades workers who built Oak Ridge have been excluded from recent federal compensation programs for former atomic workers.[25]

Workers in Oak Ridge viewed themselves both as dedicated patriots contributing to important war work and as workers whose rights were often violated by heavy-handed management. They felt that their patriotism had been taken advantage of. They had sacrificed their right to join a union and had gained nothing in return. Yet workers did not turn against the war or against patriotic rhetoric. Instead, they began to appropriate the rhetoric of patriotic service to put forward demands for rights in the workplace and the community. Health and safety risks faced by this group never became a target of protest, as turnover and shifting locations of work kept workers in the dark about exposure to radiation and other hazards.

CHAPTER 4

The World of Work

I did not wear a uniform, but I certainly lived, moved and breathed the atmosphere of a military realm.

—OLIN SMITH, 1946

DURING WORLD WAR II, the duty to maintain secrecy in the workplace at Oak Ridge was elevated to a sacred obligation. Posters and billboards throughout the city advised workers of their obligation to silence and secrecy and urged them to avoid those who would compromise the security of the installation. This propaganda was backed up by a security apparatus that included uniformed and undercover police as well as a network of informers in the plants and in the community. This system kept workers from comparing information about their jobs, including working conditions, hours, and wages.

These regulations cemented an atmosphere of "patriotic consensus" in Oak Ridge. Workers accepted them in return for high wages, steady work, and the chance to live in a better community than the one from which they had come. Though military decisions about community affairs could (and were) questioned by workers, the line was drawn at the plant gate—talking about the workplace to outsiders, even to one's family, was out of the question. The security check, the loyalty oath, the termination for security reasons were all a part of wartime workers' lives in Oak Ridge. These rules would persist into the postwar era at Oak Ridge, and many former workers at the facility still refuse to talk about their work in detail for fear of security investigation and from a sense of patriotic obligation to remain silent.

Oak Ridge's security system was based on a policy of "compartmentalization," used to keep information in one part of the project isolated. This system served several functions. While ostensibly developed to limit espionage by America's enemies (and allies, such as the Soviet Union), it also placed total control of the project firmly in the hands of General Groves and the U.S. Army, keeping project scientists, engineers, managers, or workers from questioning project policies. Finally, this policy gave Groves a great deal of personal power within the hierarchy, allowing him to rule over his empire of plants, laboratories, troops, and employees.

The level of army control workers felt depended greatly on the job they held in Oak Ridge. Those building the plants and the city's structures enjoyed much more control over their work than those who would live and work in the city once it was built. Construction workers worked a shorter stint at Oak Ridge, belonged to local trade unions, and had greater control over their work on the job site. Production and maintenance workers, however, lived and worked in a far more restrictive system, dominated by the security system.

Compartmentalization of Work in the Plants

Within the plants, the compartmentalized and secretive nature of work ensured that workers did not know much about the plant outside of their own job. Workers at Y-12 were classified by number according to where they could go in the plant and how much they were allowed to know about their job. Those at level one were limited to maintenance work in the basement. The process workers at level two were allowed on the main factory floor to work their "cubicle," though not to know what they were processing. Supervisors and engineers up to level three and four knew more about the process but were uninformed about the ultimate goals of the project. As one worker at Y-12 remembered, these work rules helped create a divided workforce: "The heater operators and the vacuum operators, they just had a 1 on their badge, and they couldn't come upstairs. The vacuum people in the basement and the heater people that operated the heaters, they couldn't come up on the top floor where the cubicles were. They had a guard at the stairs."[1]

At K-25, badge colors indicated the range of workers' movement within the plants. One woman remembered, "This is my husband's badge. It has three colors on it. Now, he was allowed to go in . . . where he worked in the conditioning building, and to the cafeteria and a color to the restroom. And we were not allowed to go anywhere else. . . . We were just in our little compartments." This structure for every part of work life, down to which bathroom one could use, was rigorously enforced within the factories. One worker recalled, "That was really how they kept that compartmentalization. That's what they called it, the way they kept it secret, because people really couldn't put things together." Even those in the next highest badge level, which included engineers, scientists, and managers, were restricted by these regulations. As an engineer recalled, "They very carefully discouraged any conversations between projects, like between Chicago-Berkeley plutonium program and Y-12, and then between X-10 and Y-12, and also on the diffusion side. That compartmentalization worked remarkably well."[2]

This system of compartmentalization limited communications between workers, as well as scientists and engineers. It ensured that even when people did have an idea about what the goal of the Manhattan Project was, they could not piece together information about the different plants and facilities involved. As a result, only a few top officials knew all of the information, and the vast majority of workers had little knowledge, and therefore little power, to question management in the factories. Those accused of violating project security were terminated from employment. The head of a laboratory section recalled that security concerns pervaded the workplace and became self-enforcing: "Being in the supervisory end of the business, a military man would come up and he would introduce himself. He would say that anything I would see that needed to be reported, I could give him the information and the source would never be told. . . . This was very common on the job and every once in a while a person would be terminated. A good worker would come up in tears, but we would never know why. . . . It was so ingrained in us that even we would question a person that we thought shouldn't be there." One foreman recalled that his wife worked as a guard at the Y-12 facility, and that "people [were] taken in for questioning and then disappeared" from Oak Ridge, as they were fired for security reasons and evicted from project housing. He thought he had an intelligence officer in his crew—"a highly educated man who went around checking batteries"—who was assigned that task to send him throughout the facility to eavesdrop on workers' conversations.[3]

The security system affected workers both inside and outside the plants, as all public spaces were monitored. One worker recalled, "Everyone had to wear a badge. And even if you walked out on the streets and went to a movie, you should wear a badge. And you were stopped at the gates going into the city to make sure that you had your badge, or you could get a pass for someone." Security personnel monitored meetings of more than three people on the streets, and undercover agents mingled with the public at social occasions. This required a small army of security personnel, and MED documents show that there were at least 18 full-time undercover intelligence agents at Oak Ridge, 178 full-time intelligence and security personnel, and 866 military guards in the community and installations.[4]

Mundane activities were also used to keep tabs on employees. At the Oak Ridge Post Office, the security system was part of routine mail delivery. One postal worker recalled that the workers at the office "recorded magazines received and the point of origin of letters, for FBI and military intelligence." Another post office employee remembered that ordinary people in Oak Ridge sent reports to military intelligence by sending letters to "Acme Credit Corporation." At the post office, many such letters arrived daily for this bogus company.[5]

Other employees confirm that the security system prevented open communication between workers about job-related issues. One man recalled, "After a while, you got so used to the thing, and the security program was so successful, you just had no desire to talk about it [or its product]." The implicit threats of the system—losing one's job, being evicted from Oak Ridge, and being drafted by the military—kept workers quiet. As one employee remembered, one "didn't mind keeping quiet because the alternative was getting shipped overseas." Off-site events could have an adverse affect on workers as well. "Someone [with my name] wrote a letter to *Daily Worker*," one worker said. "I was called in for questioning—I couldn't figure out why until afterward." This security system served, during the war, to keep workers isolated, and after the war, it continued to let workers know that their job depended on keeping quiet.[6]

The army required a signed loyalty oath to work at Oak Ridge during the war, and the standard loyalty form and background check became prerequisites for employment there. The job of screening out possible criminals and subversives fell to U.S. Army Intelligence. However, the wartime demand for labor, and the extent of employee turnover, made thorough background investigations almost irrelevant, as in many cases, it could take longer to investigate someone than they might work at the facility. Some workers held their jobs at Oak Ridge for a considerable period of time before their past records came to the attention of the authorities. In the security files of the project, the few cases of workers fired for past criminal activity are notable for the level of crime required for dismissal. Offenders dismissed from the project included workers convicted of "larceny and the white slave act," "theft, burglary, vagrancy and Mann Act," "three arrests for narcotics, 9 other arrests," and one man arrested "119 times for bootlegging." Oak Ridge's employers were more concerned with workers jumping from job to job at the facility, breaking federal manpower regulations, than they were concerned about past crime or possible Nazi or Communist influence. Yet the security apparatus was set up to screen out all kinds of problems, from those breaking manpower regulations to those whose beliefs were deemed "subversive" by Intelligence officers.[7]

This extensive security system naturally failed to prevent all crime or disruptive behavior in Oak Ridge. Reading a sample of arrest statistics, it is clear that residents and workers carved out their own spaces for unauthorized activities. As Oak Ridge was located in a "dry" area, military police fought a losing battle with project bootleggers, arresting sixty-seven people for illegal selling of alcohol or black market trade in cigarettes. Stealing other people's or government property accounted for twenty-nine arrests. Twenty-six people were charged with drunk and disorderly conduct and sixteen for drinking on the job. Assaults and felonious assaults led to twenty-one arrests. In this sample, only seven residents were arrested on morals charges such as sodomy, sex in public, and Mann Act violations, suggesting that project police cracked down harder on socially disruptive crimes than unobtrusive lawbreaking. There were some limits, apparently, to what project security sought to accomplish.[8]

Hazardous Duty on the Homefront

Production and maintenance workers in the city's three major plants— X-10, Y-12, and K-25—felt the security system most sharply. For these workers, the workplace was defined by having little control over their work and by a high degree of secrecy and compartmentalization. While their work was designed to be Taylorized, with management in control of the subdivided work process, it still required skill and attention to detail. Operators needed to have extensive training and followed a set of complicated procedures in order to process uranium to its maximum concentration. They were responsible for the complex starting procedures and for adjustment of equipment for varying conditions. At the Y-12 electromagnetic separation plant, the work done by women had previously been done by graduate students in physics at the University of California, Berkeley. However, the women who worked at Oak Ridge, by all accounts, ran the machines better, producing a purer product. As an Oak Ridge engineer recalled, "Nobody had ever operated one of those units except a Ph.D. in physics or an M.S. in engineering at Berkeley. . . . Those women operators, who were mostly high school graduates, some had never done anything before. . . . But once they got over the shock, they could sit in front of that cubicle and be the most patient person in the world. With a really small amount of supervision, they really did the electromagnetic process."[9]

The work environment at Oak Ridge alienated many workers, because of both the vast scale of the operation and the strange conditions created by the electricity and magnetism that saturated the Y-12 facility. Photographs of the workplace show great canyons of machines manned by a few women monitoring the equipment for the electromagnetic or chemical processing of uranium (fig. 7). "We were told to get these operators used to the great noise and the sparking . . . because it was frightening," one trainer recalled. "[There was so strong a magnetic field] you couldn't wear bobby pins." An engineer remembered, "I had seen girls break into tears, just walking into the building and seeing all those giant pumps and cranes and noise and everything." These feelings of discomfort were not limited to women process workers. An engineer recalled, "We had mechanics . . . who would not go into the magnetic field, because they'd feel it tugging at their keys in their pocket, and they were afraid." Nevertheless, the infor-

These jobs, monitoring electromagnetic separation machines in Y-12, were common for women in Oak Ridge, c. 1945. Box 23, Binder 69, RG 434-OR, Still Pictures Branch, NARA.

mation that would have allowed workers to understand the work environment better was kept from them.[10]

Managers went to great lengths to keep workers from learning scientific or technical information about their jobs. One trainer at Y-12 recalled, "I didn't know what everything meant about a cubicle or a track at all. I wasn't supposed to ask any questions. All I was supposed to do is to get the proper readings on certain needles." Workers were instructed to keep the needle at a certain point on the meter, but there were no clues on the machines as to what was being processed. Connie Bolling, a Y-12 operator, recalled, "I didn't tell [people] anything [about my job]. I had them ask me 'What is this? What does this stand for.' I would not answer. I'd say, 'I don't know.' Because many did answer questions and say things or even get what it is, and they were gone the next day." One engineer remembered, "The electrical groups would go through there and they'd put shunts on the meters, so as far as the girls were concerned, the meters were always reading the same ratio.... As the quality increased, we would shunt one of the meters so they would always read the same thing for them." As long as the women kept the needle between the two lines provided, they needed to know no more about the process going on within the machine.[11]

Like the Y-12 electromagnetic separation plant, the K-25 gaseous diffusion plant employed both men and women in uranium separation. This process took gaseous uranium hexafluoride, a heavy and corrosive gas, and ran it through a separation process within a system of sealed pipes. At K-25, much of the work involved maintenance of the massive system of pipes and stoppage of any leaks of air into the system. One worker recalled her task as a constant search for problems. She remembered, "I worked in the conditioning plant at K-25. [We would look for a leak] and then we'd mark it, call the inspector, and she would come inspect the leak and see if it were really leaking. Then we'd call the millwright and he'd take the pipe away. And we did this all day long to make sure the pipes were tight, to go over to the big building.... I didn't know what they were doing with these pipes." This work was often done in uncomfortable quarters, and what little workers were told about the plant raised issues of whether working in the plant was unsafe. Y-12 worker Colleen Black remembered, "In another part of it, they called it the basement, they were doing converters. I don't know exactly what they were doing, but sometimes they would send me down there to find leaks, and you had to climb up real high . . . and you had to climb all over these pipes and find the leak. I didn't know what we were doing. I didn't ask. I know one time one of the GIs told me, 'If you ever smell anything, get out of here.' So I thought, something must be going through these pipes that smells bad."[12]

Even with little information, some workers lived in fear of accidents or other problems in the plants. "The first two or three years I was damned scared," one worker recalled of the war years. "I worked hard, conscientiously. There were times when I was scared when I thought about the project —possible explosions, etc., for no one knew what was going on. But the duties I was assigned to, the things at hand, I was not afraid to do. Never at any time was I negligent or careless."[13]

Workers were not informed about possible uranium or fluorine poisoning at K-25 because of security regulations. As one trainer recalled, "It was a challenge to train [K-25 operators] adequately, make them understand the importance of leaks in the plant, the importance of keeping things in a steady state and smooth operating, without really explaining what it was we were doing and why exactly some of these things needed to be done. Also, the safety problems. You know, these are hazardous gases, and so a lot of attention was paid to that, without people getting overly concerned about it." If employees were given too much information, managers feared, recruitment and turnover would become an even bigger headache. Workers, in both construction and production, were routinely placed in situations in which exposure to radiation or other hazardous substances was possible. However, they were never given a choice to refuse a hazardous assignment or told their exposure level. They learned about the hazards of their work only retroactively, if at all.[14]

Production workers at Oak Ridge faced a working environment far different from that faced by construction and other skilled workers. More isolated in their jobs, and more tightly managed by the companies, these workers had fewer opportunities to organize or resist managerial directives. Many of them were exposed to radiation or chemicals for longer periods of time, but the lack of union representation meant that workplace health and safety policies were set without their input, and exposure occurred without their knowledge.

CHAPTER 5

"Could Be Eaten without Harm"
Scientists, Physicians, and Worker Health and Safety

IN MARCH 1945, Ebb Cade, an African American cement truck driver, fractured his arms and leg in a traffic accident, putting him in the Oak Ridge hospital. While there, the Manhattan Project Medical Division selected Cade to be a subject in the first plutonium injection experiments, to test the dangers of the new element inside the human body. Code named HP-12 by the MED, Cade was injected with 4.7 micrograms of plutonium in April and monitored for adverse effects. When his bones were set, samples were taken for biopsy, and when his teeth and gums were found to be infected, fifteen were extracted and tested for plutonium residue. Cade was never asked his consent to participate in the experiment and was never told what happened to him. Instead, he simply left the hospital on his own power and disappeared, leaving the MED without its experimental subject. He died in 1953 in North Carolina of a heart attack.

The Ebb Cade case raises critical issues about the Manhattan Project and worker safety during World War II. First, it brings up the issue of informed consent, the principle, established before World War II, that holds that those who bear the risks of medical experiments should be given a choice about their participation. Second, it raises the issue of how project medical personnel viewed workers such as Cade—as people or as "human product" for experiments? Third, Cade's case raises the issue of race and racism, and how some groups of subjects were viewed by the MED as less valuable than others.

When the federal government's Advisory Committee on Human Radiation Experiments report reached the public in 1995, it revealed that there were many cases like Cade's. There was outrage that these experiments had occurred, but little effort to put the experiments into a broader context. Cases of experimentation were part of a larger program of workplace safety, and Oak Ridge's atomic facilities were part of a larger experiment of worker exposure to hazards. Unlike the wartime Nazi and Japanese experiments on humans, Oak Ridge's tests on Cade had the intention of setting safe exposure levels of plutonium for workers. The scientists and physicians involved were driven by the goal of protecting workers as much as possible, given the constraints of production. Despite these good intentions, the MED failed to protect worker health adequately, failed to correct problems that caused injury to workers, and failed to provide information to workers about their exposure and hazards in the workplace.[1]

Workplace Hazards and Normal Accidents

Official histories of the Manhattan Project and postwar period have maintained that workers were exposed to a minimum of radiation, that standards were set according to the best contemporary knowledge of radiation effects, and that radiation injuries were minimized. However, day-to-day shop-floor and laboratory safety practice have gone unexamined in any detail in these histories because most of the pertinent documents have been classified or unavailable until recently. Workers have been reluctant to speak about their experiences on the job, out of patriotism as well as fear of employer retaliation. Recent releases of formerly classified documents, and testimony of workers to the Department of Energy, give a different, more disturbing picture of workplace safety at Oak Ridge. As the patriotic consensus about work at Oak Ridge has broken down in the 1980s and 1990s, workers have come forward to tell their stories about decades of exposure to radiation, chemicals, and other hazards.[2]

The processes undertaken at Oak Ridge were so dangerous that they were an accident waiting to happen. Charles Perrow, in his book *Normal Accidents*, defined certain technological systems as inherently hazardous and catastrophe-prone, including atomic weapons and nuclear power systems. These systems are complex, ill-understood, and lead to unpredictable and disastrous events. According to Perrow, the question is not if a disaster will occur, but where and when. The production system for nuclear weapons at Oak Ridge fits all of Perrow's criteria of a truly dangerous undertaking.[3]

Rather than possessing one set of hazards, such as uranium or petrochemicals, facilities at Oak Ridge contended with multiple toxins and hazards, including fluorine, uranium, plutonium, mercury, and beryllium.

Processes in the plants combined in different permutations, with the extra hazards of radiation thrown in as well. Dangers stemming from electrical, fire, and heat hazards were also part of the everyday work environment. Oak Ridge always was poised on the brink of an accident, whether a spill of a chemical on a worker's clothing, dust released into the plant atmosphere, radiation absorbed by skin, or tiny pieces of radioactive or toxic metal cutting skin and remaining inside the wound. The invisibility and undetectability of many of these injuries only made the system more dangerous. Unlike a fire or electrical accident, a radiation accident could go undetected.

These hazards were unevenly distributed throughout Oak Ridge's facilities. Some areas, such as the track areas of Y-12, held little risk of exposure to chemicals or radiation because radioactive substances were circulating inside machines and pipes, untouched by human hands. However, the image presented of these areas can be misleading, as in many other areas contact with hazards was a daily occurrence. For every "safe" area, there were many other support areas—where machines were disassembled and cleaned, where material was machined or mixed, where pipes had burst or substances had spilled—that forced workers to handle, breathe, or otherwise ingest hazardous substances.

Given this range of hazards, it is difficult to understand how project physicians and scientists could address these hazards to worker health. Without the power to shut down the production process, how did these project personnel justify their role in the project? Scientists and physicians' attempts to protect worker health and safety within Oak Ridge facilities represent a case study of what sociologist Diane Vaughan has called the "normalization of deviance," in which decisions about safety become embedded in a bureaucratic system that defines risks as "acceptable." The elements Vaughan describes as leading to the normalization of deviance at the National Aeronautics and Space Administration (NASA)—the culture of production and of structural secrecy—existed in the Manhattan Project and Atomic Energy Commission as well.

According to Vaughan, the normalization of deviance does not mean that officials in these organizations are guilty of amoral or evil behavior. In fact, Health Physics and Medical Division officials at Oak Ridge facilities attempted, but ultimately failed, to protect worker safety. In spite of rising concerns about worker exposure to radiation and hazardous chemicals, these risks were defined as acceptable within the context of need for rapid production of atomic materials. Scientists and physicians involved in protecting workers' health justified their role in terms of doing their best and keeping exposures to a minimum, yet they did not address the intrinsic and uncontrollable dangers of atomic weapons production. Up the chain of command, the need to produce and justify the facility weighed heavier than arguments about worker safety.[4]

Radiation Dangers
KNOWLEDGE AND DENIAL

Scientists and physicians knew that radioactive substances were dangerous in the workplace well before the start of World War II. The experience of luminous dial factories, where watch faces were painted with radioactive paint, served as a strong warning to the Manhattan Project. In the 1920s, several female dial painters died, and others were permanently injured as a result of ingesting radium paint. MED's Medical Division reports demonstrate that officials knew that radium and other radioactive substances were harmful if ingested or inhaled, that radioactive dust or gas in the air could cause lung cancer, and that overexposure to radiation could cause tissue damage and, in high doses, death by radiation sickness. Prizewinning biologist Hermann Muller's contemporarily well-known 1927 article, "The Artificial Transformation of the Gene," established that genes were damaged by radiation at low doses, and the National Council on Radiation Protection (NCRP) accepted this damage as real but unavoidable if use of radioactive materials and processes were to increase.[5]

Officials and physicians in the Manhattan Project's Health Physics and Medical Divisions created a research program to better understand radiation's effects on human tissue. The Medical Division was staffed by academic and industrial physicians (from companies such as DuPont, Monsanto, and Union Carbide), and it intensively researched the effects of radiation on biological systems. By 1944, the division reported its first findings about the effects of radiation: the substances workers were exposed to at Oak Ridge were more harmful than originally had been thought.

Manhattan Project scientists learned through animal experimentation that exposure to uranium and plutonium were harmful. A 1944 "Special Hazard Survey" listed the effects of uranium: "'Nephritis'—eating away of bone and tissue, . . . Toxic if injected into body, . . . Damage to kidney, . . . Damage to central nervous system. . . . 'Reported blood changes,' . . . chronic poisoning, which is the problem which we might meet industrially.'" On March 29, 1945, Robert Stone, associate director of the Medical Division, summarized the latest experimental finding: "We have shown that lymphomatous tumors (leukemia) can be produced by deposited strontium in the body, as well as by x-ray, gamma rays and neutrons. Also that lung (cancer) tumors can be caused by x-rays and gamma rays, and this makes possible production of tumors by alpha rays from product (plutonium) much more likely. Bone tumors are appearing in animals injected with strontium; ovarian tumors have appeared in animals being irradiated." Stone did not believe that these short-term effects were the only ones possible. "All of these have been produced in a relatively short time by relatively large doses," he wrote. "Just what doses will be required with longer exposures is not yet known." Based on the exigencies of wartime, the Medical Division postponed research on the long-term effects of radiation.[6]

Stone believed that the finding that radiation exposure causes cancer had direct implications for the project. "All of these possibilities and others have been suspected by us, but now we have shown that they are realities, and that in case of people with overexposure we will have to admit the possibility of a connection between the employment and the disease and accept the responsibility," he noted. Even after the war's close, the Manhattan Project would not admit publicly that radiation was a workplace hazard, primarily out of fear that project workers would not wish to be exposed to these substances and that those who had been exposed working for the project would sue for damages.[7]

Stone admitted that other health effects of radioactive substances were still not known. He wrote, "We have not established the permissible amounts of radioactive elements, which can be allowed to exist in a person's body without danger of complications. . . . The establishment of safe levels of air contamination for product and fission products, for safe levels of exposure to other heavy radioactive elements, whether transuranic or below uranium, remain yet to be established with any degree of certainty." He warned that the effects of radiation were often unpredictable: "As an example of the need for the studies which we have under way, I would like to point out two findings which differed markedly from our calculations. First, radiostrontium we knew would be deposited in bone and we therefore thought that bone marrow and bone tumors would be most likely. We have found that lymphomatous tumors and leukemia were in reality the first to appear. This means that we will have to expect leukemias rather than bone tumors as a subacute and chronic result of strontium. We expected from calculations based on the energy of product . . . would be 1/50 as toxic as radium. We have found that the acute toxicity of product is almost the same, gram for gram, as radium." These findings, however, did not impact safety standards for fear of a slowdown of production, as the project raced to finish the atomic bombs.[8]

The army formulated radiation safety standards for workers with uranium and plutonium production needs in mind. Military and political considerations drove the Manhattan Project, and the leadership's priority was
to finish the project before the end of the war. Hymer Friedell, head of the
Medical Division, wrote that standards for radiation exposure needed to
be set "as low as is reasonably possible" but not at levels so low that they
might "impede the production program." This "culture of production" was
not the ideal context in which to develop or enforce safety standards, and
it set a precedent for postwar practices.[9]

Leonard Cole, an MED health official, wrote critically that "MD's [on
the project] did not allow for the fact that there was a war on and insisted
upon peacetime standards of safety." The 1945 TEC Process Division
Annual Report began, "In the early part of the year, all efforts were devoted
to getting out maximum protection by forcing people and equipment to
the breaking point." The exigencies of wartime led the leadership of the
Manhattan Project and its Medical Division to accept radiation standards
that they knew were questionable. The Medical Division learned that the
"tolerance dose" set by the project of 0.1 Roentgen (R) per day was actually not as safe as first believed. In December 1943, the project's Central
Safety Commission met to discuss radiation health policy. Robert Stone
told the assembled scientists that ".1 R is definitely the maximum [allow-
able exposure], and we should strive to obtain lower exposure. Even .1 R
has shown definite changes [in blood chemistry]. . . . 1 R over twenty-four
hours produces no change, but some evidence exists to indicate .1 R exposure [delivered over] shorter periods causes some damage." Physicians realized that the project's standards were not as safe as had originally been
believed. Yet even these questionable standards were difficult to maintain
in the face of pressure to maximize production of radioactive materials.[10]

The physicians and scientists working to develop safety standards in
the 1940s took seriously their role in protecting human health, but the
demands of the production system framed serious safety hazards as acceptable risks, even when potentially life-threatening. In this context, those in
charge of safety in Oak Ridge tried to address facility safety hazards but
found their advice ignored by managers up the chain of command.[11]

What Scientists Believed about Health and Safety Policy

Waldo Cohn, a scientist at X-10, believed that the project had more than
enough information to set radiation standards. He recalled that before World
War II, "radiologists at the time knew about the dangers of radiation. . . . It

goes without saying that if you could kill cancer cells with radiation, you could also kill normal cells. We were always aware of the hazards. After all, the radium dial painter studies were back in the 1920s, and my boss at Harvard was the person who discovered that, so I was aware of the effects of radiation on living matter."[12]

Cohn also believed that the actions taken by the project to enforce safety regulations were effective: "We were very much aware of radiation hazards and what the standards were. We had all kinds of instruments and devices that were always telling us what we were being exposed to, and those things were being monitored every day—film badges, for instance." Cohn believed strongly that the project succeeded in protecting workers, telling an interviewer, "We took every reasonable precaution to stay out of those [situations where workers would be exposed to radiation], and didn't do things that would expose anyone to radiation."[13]

Another project scientist recalled that at the beginning of the war, medical knowledge of the subject was incomplete. Oak Ridge health physicist Karl Morgan remembered, "We were sort of working in the dark and taking big risks, which we should not have taken, without knowing better what we were doing." Though basic information was available in the medical literature, it did not help a project that needed to use tons of radioactive substances. "There wasn't much literature that was helpful," Morgan recalled. "All we found, essentially, might be listed under the meager information on the speculation that radium dial painters had a higher instance of cancer than would normally be expected." The only other information was "a fair amount of data—a few score of papers—that related to skin erythema [skin redness caused by radiation exposure]."[14]

Morgan's concern about skin contamination led him to conduct radiation exposure experiments on himself and workers at Y-12. He convinced twelve women who worked at Y-12, "meter readers" and nurses, to put a patch of radioactive phosphorus-32 against their skin. Morgan then monitored how long it took for their skin to become red and irritated. He later realized that this experiment was based on faulty assumptions about radioactivity: "We thought the skin erythema dose would be like sunburn on your arm—and no one worried about that at the time." Morgan, in hindsight, admitted that animal studies would have been more appropriate, but that the pressure of wartime made him seek a quick answer to his scientific and safety questions.[15]

As the project progressed, Morgan realized dangers stemmed not just from radiation, but from a whole series of hazards related to atomic production. He recalled, "We had sort of an anomaly with uranium—it was the only radionucliotide where it appeared that the chemical risk was equal or even greater than the radiation risk. The data seemed to indicate that uranium as a metal was very toxic. It went to the kidneys, some to the liver, a little to the bone, but mostly to the kidneys." Nevertheless, this knowledge of greater hazards did not lead to an end to radiation experimentation on human at Oak Ridge.[16]

With greater recognition of the hazards of the substances used by the Manhattan Project, experimentation on humans at Oak Ridge also became more extensive. Morgan recalled hearing about the case of Ebb Cade, an African American Oak Ridge truck driver who became the subject of a plutonium injection experiment. He remembered another project official telling him, "Remember that nigger truck driver that had the accident some time ago. . . . He was rushed to the military hospital in Oak Ridge and has multiple fractures . . . so this was an opportunity we had been waiting for. We gave him large does by injection of Pu-239 [plutonium]." It is telling that in the case of Ebb Cade case, no scientist spoke up or spoke out against the experiment. Like any other worker on the project, scientists were bound by the same rules of secrecy and silence in the name of the wartime cause.[17]

Case Study in Safety Practices
BUILDING 706-C

Each month, Clinton Laboratories (also known as X-10) processed tons of uranium slugs to create mere grams of plutonium. This long, frustrating process involved more than fourteen hundred employees. The volume and rate of production limited safety considerations and effectively made it impossible to limit workers' exposure to radiation. Due to a lack of time, space, and adequate personnel levels to rotate workers properly, worker safety was subordinated to production needs. Though Medical and Health Physics Division personnel brought the problem of worker overexposure to the attention of their superiors and demanded changes in laboratory procedure, production considerations put off these improvements indefinitely.[18]

One of the safety problems at Building 706-C, one of the buildings of X-10, was that the laboratory used levels of radiation above those for which it had been designed. The X-10 section chief for fission products wrote in January 1945 that 706-C was "terribly overcrowded for work of high urgency, that work is being done in the building at a level . . . in excess of design with respect to curies of hard gamma emitter and mass of uranium." Waldo Cohn, X-10's chemistry section leader, wrote, "706-C was designed for a maximum of 80 Curies [of radiation] at a point, and 10 Curies of hard gamma (it is a one slug building) and a maximum of 10 men. It is being used for 400 curies of hard gamma production on a 2300 slug basis, and it is populated by over 20 men. Janitorial and laboratory assistance is not in proportion to need in spite of effort to procure it. The pressure to produce is antagonistic to the slowness and care with which we should prefer to operate on such super-hot material." This lack of space and personnel meant that workers received overdoses of radiation.[19]

Manhattan Project records reveal that overexposure, and near-tolerance-level exposure, to radiation occurred often in the building. The Medical and Health Physics Divisions fought a constant losing battle to keep radiation levels at the project's tolerance dose. In November 1944, Dr. John E. Wirth complained that the conditions in 706-C were leading to overexposure of personnel. "It is necessary to bring certain information to your attention regarding slight over-exposure (based on a tolerance of 100mr/ day) of personnel to radiation in the 706C building during the recent hot runs," he wrote. "Analysis shows . . . 11 persons with readings greater than 100 mr/day upon one or more occasions." Waldo Cohn explained that these exposures were caused by the speed and volume of production: "All 706-C operations, to this date, have been conducted under pressure. To do our job, and to get it done, means taking calculated risks."[20]

The extent of radiation exposure in 706-C and in all of X-10 was underestimated because of failure to monitor workers with hand or personal dosimeters (radiation detectors) during routine operations. Health Physics Division reports indicate that on several occasions, hand meters or film badges were not worn or that readings were not recorded in order to keep up the rate of production. A former worker at X-10 testified that in 1945, the radiation monitoring and safety system was ineffective:

> When I went to work there we had problems with the Geiger counter. We had one assigned to the department for each shift and half the time it wouldn't work. But we still had to carry on. It didn't change the shift procedure because we were on a production schedule. [At X-10,] we didn't know what a tolerance [dose] was when I went to work there. Our dosimeters didn't work half the time, they changed different styles. We've even had dosimeters assigned to us that didn't have film in them.

This lack of proper badges and safety equipment implies that there was systematic undercounting of worker radiation exposure.[21]

The problems at X-10 led project medical personnel to question the overall validity of the MED's radiation standards. Dr. Wirth wrote, "The tolerance dose is based not on definite facts and observed reactions following measured amounts of radiation over long periods of time, but rather on clinical impressions or some partially observed reactions following amounts of radiation which can only be grossly estimated. . . . There is an attempt to allow a wide margin for safety to the individual based on continued exposure, but this does not consider genetics to any great extent." He justified exposing workers to this much radiation because "it seems impossible to handle such large quantities of active materials with existing facilities with any fewer over-exposures."[22]

Chemical Contamination in Departments 185 and 186

The Y-12 plant, managed by Tennessee Eastman Corporation, contained some of the most severe occupational hazards in Oak Ridge. Y-12's primary mission was electromagnetic separation of uranium—women watching and adjusting cyclotrons that separated U-235 and U-238. For the most part, this work isolated employees from the hazardous substances inside the machines they tended. However, Y-12's secondary function, chemical recovery (also known in TEC as Beta Recovery or Departments 185 and 186), involved a far higher level of workplace exposure to chemicals and radiation. Chemical recovery workers, women and men, faced almost daily hazards from the harsh acids used to remove tiny bits of uranium from pieces of machinery and the subsequent processing of the mixture to separate out the uranium and convert it back to a usable form (fig. 8). Workers in this division handled radioactive materials, acids, and other chemicals in vats and open tanks. Contemporary photographs show that these departments were crowded with pipes, hoses and tanks, with many points of potential contact for workers and hazardous substances.

The hazards faced in chemical recovery at Y-12 were as dangerous or more dangerous than any faced in X-10. TEC did not do an adequate job of protecting worker safety, by admission of its own medical and safety departments. Instead, TEC had an extensive history of occupational injury and disability that has only recently been declassified. These problems in the chemical recovery section of Y-12 were known to TEC's Medical and Safety Departments, but production pressures and lack of resources given these departments ensured that poor working conditions in the recovery areas of the plant remained a source of worker injuries until the plant's shutdown in 1947.[23]

As a result of Manhattan Project animal and human experimentation, TEC knew about the medical and safety challenges of radiation. Its Medical and Safety Departments attempted, without success, to convince supervisors and managers at TEC that the substances Y-12 processed were dan-

These women are working in chemical recovery operations, c. 1945.
Box 23, Binder 69, RG 434-OR, Still Pictures Branch, NARA.

gerous. In December 1943, Dr. James Sterner, medical director of TEC, warned that animal studies should not reassure project officials that inhaled radioactive substances were safe at low doses. He wrote that "not every case that has had a very slight exposure will be hospitalized, but unless we have more convincing data than the animal studies, we intend to place at rest those individuals in whom we expect an appreciable exposure." Sterner also worried that pulmonary edema might go undetected if those exposed were not hospitalized.[24]

Despite Sterner's misgivings, TEC ran Y-12 as though it were facing only conventional hazards such as those found in the company's other industrial chemical plants. For instance, TEC did not request insurance through the MED for exposure to "special hazards." W. E. Kelley of the U.S. Army Corps of Engineers relayed to TEC that "all concerned are of the opinion that the exposure is such as encountered in any normal chemical manufacturing plant and that there is no extra hazard requiring special coverage." This determination could only reinforce the complacency toward health and safety within the organization and put an official stamp of approval on a dangerous policy.[25]

In April 1944, TEC circulated a memo, "General Precautions in Handling T Material," informing managers of uranium's toxicity. The memo noted that "T," uranium, was toxic if ingested, inhaled, or came into contact with skin or an open wound. Further, it communicated that the standards for inhalation of uranium had been "arbitrarily" set at the same level as lead, and it suggested that respirator use was "imperative" when any of the substance was airborne.

Despite these clear warnings, TEC's managers and supervisors, particularly on the shop floor, showed an ignorance and carelessness not found elsewhere in Oak Ridge. TEC safety official J. C. Hecker's May 1944 memo stated that "certain members of the supervision have stated that the compounds encountered in the processing are of such a low order of toxicity that considerable amounts 'could be eaten without harm.'" As a result of these attitudes, according to the memo, "there has been a laxity in the application of the safe practices which were set up to control the absorption of the potentially harmful chemicals." As the substances involved included uranium, it is clear that many TEC supervisors simply did not know or care about the substances with which they and their employees were working.[26]

Safety inspectors at TEC faced an uphill battle to address chemical and radioactive problems in the workplace. Safety inspection reports indicate that TEC knew of many dangers within Y-12 and had developed possible solutions to minimize worker exposure. However, over and over, resources were not allocated to safety—needed equipment was delayed, on order, or not available. In the meantime, work in these hazardous areas continued unabated.

Safety inspections of Department 186, conducted in February 1945, indicate that TEC management knew about ongoing safety problems in the division. Safety problems were found in many areas of the chemical recovery process. Not all employees were wearing safety glasses, fire extinguishers were so heavy that female employees would not be able to lift them in case of emergency, and respirators were stored in areas containing uranium dust, contaminating them before use. Several areas had more dramatic problems that were recognized at the time as hazardous. Room 10A of Building 9202 was found to be particularly unsafe. Inspectors documented that the "lighting and ventilation are very unsatisfactory. The regular air intake has been sealed off because of toxic fumes and a new intake has not yet been installed." Ventilation hoods also were not used properly, allowing gas to leak into the room and condensation from the hoods to drip onto employees working below. Loose mercury was found on shelves and hotplates were found in sinks, as were other harmful chemicals. According to inspectors, one laboratory in the building, Building 9733-3, Room 12, never had received a copy of the safety rules.[27]

Working conditions in Departments 185 and 186, short of space and pressed for time, meant that many hazards would persist for the duration of the war. Safety inspectors noted in their report that in Building 9202, Room 10-A, "previous safety and housekeeping reports have commented on the crowded conditions of the laboratory. The volume of work and personnel required to do the work does not permit any alteration of this situation." Another room's report noted, "The space is too small for the work being done."[28]

TEC investigations revealed that uranium was finding its way into the air at Y-12, ultimately landing in the ventilation ducts. J. M. DallaValle investigated the issue of airborne T at Y-12, seeking to both cut down on worker exposure and increase the yield of the plant. He wrote, based on his investigation, "The presence of large amounts of T in many cases was confirmed. Considering the amount of deposit found, the total quantities lost through ventilation must be enormous (relatively speaking)." In building 9202, DallaValle found problems such as a minimum of 1.1 kilogram/day of uranium dust escaping production, finding its way onto horizontal surfaces, into ventilation ducts, and onto the clothing and into the lungs of workers there. When pieces of equipment were loaded and unloaded, the dust escaped into the air, and "the local exhaust systems . . . require overhauling." In a remarkable understatement, DallaValle concluded, "Dust concentrations in Bulk Treatment Operations constitute a potential industrial hygiene hazard."

Other areas of the plant were just as bad or worse than Bulk Processing. Charge filling operations handled uranium chloride rather than uranium oxide, making the presence of airborne chemicals more dangerous, according to DallaValle. He suggested that the area was a "serious industrial hygiene hazard" and recommended "a complete redesign of the local exhaust system." The carbon burning area of 9201-1 was declared "an industrial hygiene hazard" requiring "immediate attention." The entire facility lacked ventilation equipment equal to the standards of the day, according to DallaValle. Air filtering equipment had been installed in the building, but "no filters have thus far been inserted."[29]

While TEC medical and safety personnel attempted to keep conditions safe in these departments, safety measures simply fell behind production, and equipment needed for safety was not installed or ordered. G. C. Henderson, a TEC safety inspector, informed the company in January 1944 that ventilation hazards existed in the Chemical Division. He wrote, "At present, considerable quantities of material #723 are spilled on the floor and equipment" and noted that machinery had been ordered to improve ventilation in the facility earlier in January. He urged TEC officials "that this order be rushed," as "the machine will eliminate most of the respiratory hazard and minimize contamination of equipment and personnel." Henderson added, "Available information indicates the material being processed is of a toxic nature," and he suggested sterilization of respirators, as well as routine blood tests and urinalysis of employees every month of six weeks.[30]

Dangers were not limited to relatively small leaks. In June 1944, TEC's Chemical Production Division realized that a critical mass of atomic materials were in use in Y-12's Building 9207. J. L. Patterson of TEC wrote to the army and requested assistance, as "at present time, no provisions have been made in the 9207 area for stopping reactions resulting from bringing together by accident an unsafe quality of material." This type of accident would have put many lives in immediate harm, and the fact that the issue had not been raised earlier demonstrates that at TEC, safety concerns took a back seat to production pressures.[31]

Shortages of equipment contributed to occupational injuries at TEC. In February 1944, a worker reported to the Medical Department a few days after a possible chemical exposure. Although the workers had been told to wear gloves while working with chemicals, they noted in their memo that "up to the present, this Department still seems to be critically short of rubber gloves and other items of protective equipment. . . . Some individual complaints were heard that no adequate space is provided for keeping protective items when operators are off duty. If space is not available in the change house, some provision must be made for proper handling of these items."[32] The injury in question resulted in no time lost for the worker and therefore was not even counted as an accident in TEC's statistics.

Reports of TEC Departments 185 and 186 reveal that many worker health problems were the result of attempts to speed production. The July 1944 progress report for Department 185 announced that it had cut the time for several key steps in the process from 7.5 days to 5.0, and another from 10.5 days to 8.7. Chemical Division employees handled radioactive and chemically harmful material directly, and the shortened production time meant more speed in the workplace and opportunities for accidental exposure. In the same period that production increased and time for each batch decreased, the division suffered thirty-two "minor accidents" and six serious cases of gas exposure, two of which caused employees to lose work time and two of which required hospitalization.[33]

Departments 185 and 186 also had higher than average turnover and quit rates, requiring greater numbers of newly hired employees. In November 1944, the Chemical Process Division hired 116 workers (the entire division at the time numbered only 200), while the much larger Production Process Division needed to hire only 133. The Chemical Process Division's progress report noted that personnel who left the division mentioned "health and dislike of type of work" as the top reason for leaving, and "health" was the second most important reason."[34] None of these problems, recognized at the time, could sway TEC or the army to slow production or clean up the workplace. In the name of processing uranium, working conditions at Y-12 suffered, leading to a long list of worker injuries that TEC denied causing.

The Institutionalization of Emergency

The end of World War II did not end safety problems at Oak Ridge. Instead, the wartime experience of rushed production was institutionalized in safety standards and practices, which put Oak Ridge on "permanent emergency" status. In August 1945, J. M. DallaValle returned to Building 9206 of Y-12 and reported that the carbon burning and carbon breakup sections were still not properly ventilated, and that operations were taking place over the mouth of an open metal barrel without any extra ventilation equipment. He suggested ventilated enclosures for these operations and noted that with the dropping of the atomic bombs, attention could be turned from "matters of existing T concentrations (though ever important)" to "the provision of necessary safeguards." TEC records do not indicate that such changes took place. Instead, trapped in a rut of poor safety and handling practices, TEC never redesigned Y-12 according to the safety section's suggestions. Instead, it ran the plant as it was run during the war until the 1947 government-ordered shutdown.[35]

Building 706-C of X-10 and Departments 185 and 186 of Y-12 were not isolated problems. The hundreds of other buildings at the four facilities at Oak Ridge were part of the same culture of production and were governed by the same medical and safety policies. Unfortunately, even the end of the war did not significantly change the safety philosophy of either the companies that operated Oak Ridge or the federal government. Instead, production speed and quantity continued to be emphasized and worker safety and health remained a low priority.

CHAPTER 6

The End of the War and the Transformation of Community, 1945–1948

THE DROPPING OF THE ATOMIC BOMB answered a big question for workers at Oak Ridge but raised questions about the future of the city. Would Oak Ridge and its factories be necessary in the postwar world, or would the U.S. Army scrap the city as war surplus? Larger international and national questions affected Oak Ridge's future as well. In 1945, Congress debated whether atomic energy would be under international control or remain an American monopoly. If international control of atomic energy were implemented, as proposed under the "Lilienthal Plan," further manufacture of nuclear weapons might cease indefinitely. Congress also debated who would control Oak Ridge. Would atomic energy be under civilian or military control? Would Oak Ridge remain an army installation or under a new civilian form of governance such as the proposed Atomic Energy Commission?[1]

For residents and workers, all these questions boiled down to one: Are you staying or going home? Thousands of workers left Oak Ridge before layoffs began, while others decided to make Oak Ridge their permanent home. These individual and family decisions transformed the community from a wartime boomtown to a community. There was an upsurge in community interest and activism in the area as workers and residents began to demand a greater say in how the community was run and to assert rights that had not been permitted under the military regime.

Two public rituals mark this period of transition. The first was the celebration of the dropping of the atomic bomb on Hiroshima, and the second was the military's "E" awards ceremony, in which it acknowledged Oak Ridge contractors for efficiency during wartime. These two public rituals, one by the military and the contractors, the other by workers and scientists, marked a transition between the wartime Oak Ridge and the future and reflected the ideology and world view of each group, as well as their different definitions of patriotism. Workers conceived of their city, in the wake of the dropping of the bomb, as a workers' city proud of its role in defeating Japan. The celebration orchestrated by the army revealed the military's desire to maintain control of the social terrain of Oak Ridge, as it had during World War II. This tension between the two visions of Oak Ridge would not disappear during the postwar period but would become more pronounced.

Workers Celebrate

The dropping of the atomic bomb on Hiroshima caught Oak Ridge's workers and scientists by surprise. The *Oak Ridge Journal,* the city's official, military-controlled paper, did not publish the story for a week after the explosion. Instead, residents of Oak Ridge read about Hiroshima in the *Knoxville News-Sentinel,* sold at the special cost of one dollar to the residents of the city. One long-time resident remembered that Oak Ridgers, on hearing of the bomb's drop, claimed prior knowledge. "When I left Oak Ridge to go in the Navy," he recalled, "I had no idea of what we produced. When the bomb was dropped, I was as shocked as everyone else. I hadn't the foggiest idea. But plenty of people in Oak Ridge, after the initial shock would tell you, 'I knew it all along.'"[2]

The news of the first atomic bomb dropped at Hiroshima temporarily dissolved the social structure of Oak Ridge. As if celebrating Mardi Gras, Oak Ridgers for one night suspended the social system of the community and factory. As one resident remembers:

> I was on the evening shift. All of my operators from the cubicle room, they left their cubicles running. They left the calutrons, handlers, they all ganged out, "They dropped the bomb! We made the bomb!" They were just whooping it up out there in the middle of the top floor. Even the heater operators came up, and the vacuum operators came in. They heard about it. Everybody had just a great time, and they left those machines running! They'd kick off and they stayed off. Some of them clocked out!

In a moment, Oak Ridge's workers disregarded the security system that had been rigidly maintained at the plants since operations began. Workers from different sections of the plants all gathered on the factory floor and left for the evening without shutting down their machines. The celebration was a spontaneous walkout, a night in which those who had minded the machines for years decided to let the machines mind themselves.[3]

One employee recalled that workers were not the only ones released from factory and security regulations; scientists "were running around town, shouting, 'Uranium!' 'atomic!' All these things they had never been able to say before, they were shouting out like dirty words." The end of restrictions on information meant that finally, workers, scientists, engineers, and managers all understood the enormity of their work at Oak Ridge.

In the course of celebration, the moral and ethical dimensions of the bomb did not escape workers and scientists. A minister at Oak Ridge at the time pointed out that with the dropping of the first atomic bomb, celebrations broke out instantly in Oak Ridge, some with a virulently anti-Japanese character. But with the dropping of the second bomb, and greater knowledge of the destructiveness of the first, he recalled, "Oak Ridge was a ghost town." He remembered that there was a shift in attitudes from a spirit of celebratory "We did it " to a more introspective "What have we done?"[4]

This celebration reflected the pride that Oak Ridge workers and residents felt in helping to defeat Japan. It also reflected a desire to end the secrecy, security restrictions, and strict control of public space that had marked army rule of the city. For a short period, each of these had been temporarily held at bay by a massive public celebration. The army, however, did not intend to dismantle these structures, and they planned their own celebration to reinforce their rule of the city.

The Military-Industrial Celebration

Unlike the spontaneous celebrations of workers and scientists at the announcement of the explosion of the atomic bombs, the U.S. Army had choreographed its public celebration well in advance. The race to gain credit for winning World War II began with the close of hostilities. The army, as the owners and managers at Oak Ridge, decided to reward its contractors and workers by bestowing two separate awards, the E flag for contractors and the A lapel pin for employees. On Saturday 29, 1945, the War Department presented E flags to contractors in the first postwar public gathering at Oak Ridge. Secretary of War Robert Patterson and Gen. Leslie Groves came to Oak Ridge to preside over the ceremony. The structure of the ceremony was a reflection of the status of the participants—the army and corporate officials sat on a stage decorated with patriotic emblems and symbols, while workers and residents stood or sat on a field in front of them (figs. 9 and 10).

Celebration after workers hear news of the dropping of the atomic
bomb, c. 1945. Box 19, Notebook 58, RG 434-OR,
Still Pictures Branch, NARA.

The army's E flag was awarded ostensibly to reward labor and management for wartime cooperation. However, in the case of Oak Ridge, organized labor was given no part in the ceremony. In other plants across the country, E award ceremonies involved both management and union officials. At Oak Ridge, though, there were ten E flags, one for each of the nine honored contractors and one for all Oak Ridge workers. This tenth flag was presented to a Fercleve Corporation personnel officer rather than to a worker or union official. Thus, no workers were on stage for the ceremony, which consisted of army and company speeches.

At the ceremony, Secretary of War Patterson told the audience that "if there was one single instrument of war that brought peace to the world, it was the bomb you built here. We would have won without it, but it hastened the day of victory and saved many American lives." Patterson stressed that Oak Ridge workers, managers, and scientists had all shared in the sacrifice to build the bomb. "This was not achieved by regimentation but by voluntary cooperation," he said. "Labor gave its utmost without asking to be told the purpose of the work. Industry gave its skill and know how without patent rights or profits. Scientists gave their hope and knowledge without hope of reward."[5]

The assembled crowd for the E award, Oak Ridge's first formal
public gathering, c. 1945. Box 19, Notebook 58,
RG 434-OR, Still Pictures Branch, NARA.

General Groves told the workers, "The job you did was tremendous and inspiring. It was a job that demanded skill and determination. You went forward on faith alone; faith in your government and faith that your efforts were of the greatest importance. But faith was not enough. Hard, unremitting labor was necessary for success. Each time a scaffold was built, a nail was hammered, a building was finished, a dial was turned, it meant that you were sharing in hastening peace. Your work was and is a part of the American ingenuity which surpasses that of all other peoples." Though Groves was certainly sincere in his praise, the characteristics he found so appealing, such as workers' capacity for silent sacrifice, were already starting to change in Oak Ridge.[6]

For Oak Ridge's contractors, the public award ceremony was only the appetizer for military, corporate, and elected officials. The secretary of war, the governor of Tennessee, and the state's congressional delegation were all honored at a lunch and dinner reception sponsored by the companies that managed the construction and production at Oak Ridge. Officeholders were invited to "the Kellex Corporation luncheon to be given in honor of Mr. Patterson" as well as the "reception . . . in honor of Mr. Patterson at the Andrew Johnson Hotel at Knoxville" given by "Carbide and Carbon Chemicals Corporation, Tennessee Eastman Corporation, J. A. Jones Construction Company and Stone and Webster Engineering Corporation." The bonds of war between contractors, the military, and officeholders were celebrated in these networking events. Workers and unions were left out of this military-industrial coalition, as they were not considered important enough to be invited. However, while contractors and the army dined in Knoxville, back in Oak Ridge, workers and community residents were beginning to chafe under wartime restrictions.[7]

The Postwar Transformation

In both the community and the workplace, the end of the war transformed social relations in Oak Ridge. Workers were no longer willing to live under the army's community and workplace regulations. Instead, with the departure of those who saw Oak Ridge as a temporary home, and the decision of many workers to make Oak Ridge a permanent home, residents demanded more power at work and in the community. One resident recalled that wartime Oak Ridge was "a constant transient society," and high school students chose prom dates based on their best guess as to who would remain in town long enough to attend. With people coming and leaving quickly, little community spirit developed, and "during the war, [there was] not a lot of cross-communications with other parts of the community." But with the close of the war, she added, those who chose to stay at Oak Ridge became active in solving community problems.[8]

Employees' decision to stay or leave at the end of the war transformed Oak Ridge, and the end of the war led to a massive drop in the city's population. On September 1, 1945, there were 71,327 residents, but in the space of ninety days, this dropped to 59,499, a decline of almost 17 percent. On June 1, 1946, the population was down to a low of 43,742. This drop in population changed the character of Oak Ridge from a crowded, bustling place to a more stable, relaxed area. Many workers simply left at the end of the war to return home or seek work elsewhere. As one worker recalled,

"Some people just packed up and left the day after they found out what we were making." For most, leaving was not a decision based on moral discomfort with the bomb but a suspicion that war-related enterprises would shutting down and laying off workers, at a time when millions of servicemen would be returning home looking for work. For other workers, particularly women, the end of war meant an end to what they had always believed was temporary work. As one worker recalled, "People started leaving. . . . Some, when they heard the bomb was dropped, they left. They said, 'I'm going home. My husband will be coming home soon.'"[9]

Another resident recalled, "There was so much consideration [after the war] as to what was going to happen to Oak Ridge, whether it was going to go up or down. A lot of people were leaving with the idea that it would just become a ghost town. Others were willing to take a chance." Those who did decide to stay had made, perhaps without realizing the consequences fully, an investment in the community. "At the beginning Oak Ridge was an army base, but it gradually developed into a town," one worker remembered about the postwar period. Part of this demilitarization was a move to give residents more power and more responsibility over their lives. One resident recalled, "There was a lot of dissatisfaction. . . . For a number of years we couldn't own our own houses and we weren't at war any longer. You couldn't figure out why you had to be coddled, essentially, by the army. I mean, they supplied the electricity and painted the houses when, I think, everybody was quite ready to take care of it themselves."[10]

When people decided to stay, their interest in the political life of the community increased dramatically. "In 1945 and 1946, people were wanting to be real citizens, that's why they got so involved with politics," one resident recalled. "They were planning to stay around. They had jobs here, you see. And then the housing opened up and people could have a home here or rent a home. They wanted to stay and the children could go to school. It was beginning to become a city on its own." Out of this new sense of community came an awareness that Oak Ridge was an important part of the American defense effort and that its workers and residents deserved respect. Once people considered Oak Ridge their permanent home, they became less willing to tolerate the ill-organized community management that characterized Oak Ridge during the war. Problems with housing that were accepted as part of wartime exigencies became intolerable. Workers began to demand decent affordable housing as a right. Since the federal government was the only landlord at Oak Ridge, workers began to demand greater housing rights as patriotic citizens. In the workplace, workers began to petition for union representation, in spite of the fact that union leadership still maintained a gentleman's agreement not to support these efforts.[11]

Workers Challenge Housing Policies

While workers grumbled about Manhattan Project housing policies during the war, residents grudgingly accepted small quarters and lack of comfort as part of the patriotic effort. With the end of the war, however, they no longer wished to live in trailers or dormitories; they demanded to buy or rent houses in Oak Ridge. In this postwar period, residents argued that they had a right to housing based on patriotic World War II service—military or industrial. John F. Edwards wrote to the Atomic Energy Commission, "I would like to speak to you about the housing situation for veterans in Oak Ridge, which is very rotten. I am a veteran and have a small family, with two small kids, one of them an infant. . . . I have been ordered to move into a VC-1, which does not have any heating system at all, with the exception of an oil stove that takes 7 gallons for every 24 hour period. And then it doesn't keep it warm. Which I absolutely cannot afford at 85 cents an hour. Along with the other veterans of the city, I would like to see this matter investigated thoroughly. Give us a chance to be equal with every one." While Edwards might have accepted his new housing assignment with grumbling during the war, the end of the war meant that the government should stop expecting daily sacrifices and start rewarding him for his wartime service.[12]

Workers, fed up with the unfairness of housing allocation, complained that higher occupational groups, such as managers and engineers, received preferences for housing at the expense of blue-collar workers. This suspicion was confirmed in 1949, when two Roane-Anderson housing office employees were found to be accepting whiskey and beer in return for favorable housing assignments. However, the AEC did not admit the bribery case publicly but handled the matter quietly as a "reorganization" of the housing office.[13]

Patriotic wartime industrial service also was used as an argument to demand housing. A worker wrote about his eviction, "I am writing in regard to an injury I received while working in the Atomic Plant here. . . . I am still under a doctor's care and am unable to work. Since TEC terminated their contract here, I have been terminated. The housing authority has asked me to vacate their house by Oct 31, 1947. I feel I am unable to do so as I have no place to go. . . . As a citizen of the United States and a believer in democracy, I don't feel as though I am getting a fair deal, as I was working for TEC on a government job." Workers, who were expected to leave when they were no longer needed, resented this attitude of disposability and fought to remain in the city.[14]

Women workers also demanded the right to housing. A veteran wrote to Representative Estes Kefauver, U.S. congressman from the Oak Ridge area, that women should be recognized as the head of household when their husbands attended college full time: "There are, in Oak Ridge, many married veterans who are now attending the University of Tennessee, but who were, until recently, employed in the Oak Ridge plants. Our wives are now employed in the Oak Ridge plants, school system, etc. The housing section is refusing to allow us to continue living in the houses we now occupy, even though our wives are employed. The housing section maintains that it only rents to heads of families who are working at Oak Ridge. . . . The veterans with children, therefore, have no choice except to leave the area. . . . Such doings make one wonder about the Veterans' so called rights and privileges." Though American wives were expected to return to the home after the war, many at Oak Ridge could not afford to—and resented the government's policies that failed to recognize the worth of women's work.[15]

Women's demands were based not only on their familial status but on their individual wartime service, whether in the factories or the military. A woman resident of Oak Ridge wrote to the AEC, "I have a legal resident right to a house and a job. I am Mrs. America. My GI Bill of rights entitles me to a house and business. Would you please build a house for me on 7th street. I want a bath, living room and small library."[16] Workers housing demands, however extreme, are evidence of what residents of Oak Ridge felt entitled to after years of working six and seven day weeks and living in cramped conditions.

Service to the community was another the justification Oak Ridge residents used to demand better housing. Schoolteachers Alice Edwards and Nannie Sullivan wrote that as teachers, they had a right to year-round accommodations rather than a new dormitory room each year. "When we return from summer vacation will we be required again to deposit our belongings at the bus station while we rush madly to the housing office for handout assignments of dormitory rooms," the wrote. "Must this be a teacher's fate year after year in Oak Ridge? Why this unfair discrimination against the profession that renders such vital services to this community?"[17]

Even soldiers in the Special Engineering Detachment (SED) demanded better quarters. Many came to Oak Ridge to work temporarily in hard-to-fill civilian jobs. By 1946, however, many of these soldiers' wives worked in the plants at Oak Ridge, and the men were no longer merely soldiers temporarily stationed at Oak Ridge but semipermanent residents. SED officer J. A. Finneran complained that married enlisted men of the SED were "compelled by housing regulations to live in rented rooms or dormitories, which in my opinion is a grave injustice in view of the duties of most of these men, and of the fact that their wives are also employed on the project." Even to those in the army, military control over housing in Oak Ridge was becoming intolerable.[18]

Additionally, residents of Oak Ridge began to demand the freedom to elect local officials. In 1944, it had been difficult for Oak Ridge residents to vote, as Anderson County did not recognize them as residents. This lead to little protest within Oak Ridge, as many workers simply voted by absentee ballot in their home communities. But by 1948 workers were actively demanding voting rights and enough time off from work to fulfill them. Carbide and Carbon, under pressure from Congressman Kefauver and workers, allowed day-shift workers to leave at 3:30 P.M. (polls were open until 7:00) and let workers from surrounding communities depart work even earlier so they could drive home to vote. With the transformation of Oak Ridge from a temporary to permanent community, residents began to demand more from the federal government, basing their claims on service during the war. All their grievances had one thing in common: they were looking for a permanent home in Oak Ridge, and all demanded that the federal government treat them as citizens rather than subjects.[19]

African Americans Demand a Better Deal

White and black residents at Oak Ridge made similar demands for housing and community facilities after the close of the war. For blacks, however, changing these conditions was more difficult. As a result of the Manhattan Project's, and later the AEC's, policies of racial segregation, the African American community's demands were met with delays. To both the MED and AEC, residential integration was virtually unthinkable. Only pressure from the national African American media about the housing situation of black workers in Oak Ridge made the AEC take any notice of the situation.

Beginning on December 29, 1945, the *Chicago Defender* published a series of articles about African Americans at Oak Ridge. Its headline read "Atomic City Birthplace of Paradoxes: Negro Kids Can't Go to School at Biggest Brain Center." Enoc Waters, a *Defender* correspondent, discovered that Oak Ridge was a "city of paradoxes." He wrote, "Here, millions of dollars are marshaled to exploit the atomic theory, but not enough pennies can be corralled to provide for the welfare and comfort of a few thousand Negro workers." Waters found that most black ghettos were the remnants of housing left behind by whites, "but Oak Ridge is unique. It is the first community I have ever seen with slums that were deliberately planned. The concept back of the planning and operation of this small city is as backward sociologically as the atomic bomb is advanced scientifically. The ignorance, prejudice and fascism of one is as apparent as the knowledge, enlightenment, efficiency and patriotism that characterized the other." During wartime, no press had reported on the situation in Oak Ridge, but postwar African American journalists and readers would no longer accept these conditions as a temporary sacrifice.[20]

Waters noted that black children were attending school at a black high school in Knoxville rather than in Oak Ridge. He also noted that though the government claimed to be following "local custom" in segregating Oak Ridge, the surrounding area, particularly Knoxville, treated black citizens far better than did the army. The army, "far from adopting a 'local custom,' has in fact introduced at Oak Ridge a social pattern that is actually foreign to the area," he wrote. Though Waters may have exaggerated the local racial tolerance of white citizens, he was correct in noting that the army ran the city and had the power to desegregate it at any time.[21]

In a second article, "Negroes Live in Modern Hoovervilles at Atomic City," Waters focused on the housing complaints of local residents, pointing out that "their homes are known as hutments. A hutment is nothing more than a 16 x 16 packing box, its floor set flush to the ground. It has four unscreened unglassed apertures that serve as windows. They admit to the interior light, rain, flies, mosquitoes, and heat or cold depending on the season." The 1,050 blacks living in Oak Ridge withstood these conditions for the duration of the war because of the high wages available there, but with the close of hostilities, the situation became intolerable. As Waters wrote, the situation was, in fact, becoming better for blacks at Oak Ridge, as families were moved out of hutments and into "victory cottages," which had glass windows and were raised off the ground. Yet the fact that no blacks were offered the "attractive little frame cottages that stand vacant throughout the project" was a source of community aggravation.[22]

The Oak Ridge hutments had not always been reserved solely for African American residents; they had served early in the war as housing for both black and white workers. In 1944, when Roane-Anderson took over management of the hutment camps, there were thirty-three hundred whites (mostly single construction workers) and thirteen hundred blacks living in hutment units. In the fall of 1945, the last white hutment areas were closed down, and whites were placed in existing white dormitories or houses. To eliminate all hutments, additional housing would have to be built to accommodate Oak Ridge's African American community. African Americans were kept in the hutments well after the end of the war. In 1949, seventy-seven families were still living in hutments, as the new "colored community" had not yet been built by the AEC.[23]

Education was another area in which the AEC failed to provide adequate facilities for African Americans. While Tennessee state law precluded integrated schools in Oak Ridge, the AEC maintained an inadequate system of education for African Americans. This neglect was intentional and systematic and did not improve with the end of the war. Instead, African American pupils were warehoused in Scarboro Elementary and Secondary School, an inadequate facility built by the AEC in 1950. The building, remote from its neighborhood, was deemed to be a failure by the Oak Ridge school system, receiving a grade of 487 out of 1000 for its physical facilities. The committee found its toilets, electrical system, and heating and ventilation systems unsuitable. The small high school program at the school (thirty-three students in 1952) was judged to have a "comparatively limited curriculum" compared to white schools in Oak Ridge and was maintained by volunteer white teachers and scientists who attempted to meet the needs of the students there. The AEC had done nothing to expand educational opportunity for African Americans in Oak Ridge between 1942 and 1952. It would take the 1954 *Brown v. Kansas Board of Education* decision to move the commission toward educational equality.[24]

Circumstances did not change quickly for African Americans at Oak Ridge, even with negative publicity from the *Chicago Defender*. Instead, the racism structured into community life in the early 1940s persisted. With limited income, members of the black community found it difficult to afford new housing that would take them out of hutments and dormitories. In September 1949, LeRoy H. Jackson wrote, "It was found that there were insufficient numbers of colored people employed in Oak Ridge either in the production plants or in connection with community operations to rent these [single-family house] units." Even as the African American community became a permanent part of Oak Ridge and demanded a voice in how their community was run, blacks still were given separate and unequal housing and facilities. Until the *Brown* decision, blacks could receive only a grammar school education in Oak Ridge and were bussed to a black high school in Knoxville for further education. Residential segregation persisted in Oak Ridge even with the end of the hutments. The struggle for the black community in Oak Ridge is a story of long-term frustration, as discrimination instituted at the founding of the city took years to eradicate.[25]

Workers Challenge the Suppression of Unions

The temporary nature of Oak Ridge during the war had provided employers with a convenient excuse not to improve wages or working conditions. As one low-level manager at TEC remembered, "If you went in to ask for a pay increase, they would tell you 'Well, we're going to shut down soon, so its hardly worth fooling with.'" After the end of the war, this excuse no longer worked, and employees organized to demand higher wages, better working conditions, and representation by unions.[26]

Workers at Oak Ridge appealed for their rights to the federal agencies that regulated labor relations in America: the National Labor Relations Board and the Federal Mediation and Conciliation Service (FMCS). Based on worker complaints, the NLRB pressured the Manhattan Project for action. In September 1945, A. C. Joy, an NLRB examiner, wrote to J. J. Flaherty of the MED Labor Relations Office, "Inasmuch as the nature of the operations at Oak Ridge is now public knowledge, I assume that the previously existing security requirements no longer prevail and that we will be able to proceed to determine what representatives, if any, the employees have chosen to represent them in accordance with the NLRA [National Labor Relations Act, or Wagner Act]." The NLRB assumed that the end of the war would mean a lifting of security at Oak Ridge. The army did not see the situation the same way.[27]

Secretary of War Robert Patterson replied to the NLRB that "the continued necessity for preserving the highest degree of security with respect to all matters involving the Manhattan Project" meant that the NLRB should "continue to refrain from taking any affirmative action in cases involving it." This position would not last. Workers, unwilling to tolerate army policies against union organizing, started demanding rights that they had not sought during wartime.[28]

Firemen and Oilers Fight Wage Cuts

In October 1945, a group of workers at Carbide and Carbon threatened to strike—before their union had even been recognized by the NLRB or the company. On October 12, the Firemen and Oilers Union at Oak Ridge sent a telegram to the NLRB, requesting a strike vote at "Carbide and Carbon

Corp.,—Now known as atomic bomb plant." Members of the Firemen and Oilers International Brotherhood were prepared to strike for union recognition by Carbide and Carbon. The union had handled grievances without a formal agreement with the company since 1943, but with the end of the war, the union demanded to be officially recognized.[29]

In January 1946, with no resolution of the problem, the Firemen and Oilers International Brotherhood sought to strike to protest a 20 percent wage cut at Carbide and Carbon. However, the company refused to negotiate with the union at all, based on the earlier War Department refusal to recognize unions at Oak Ridge. Union members then sent a telegram to President Truman, asking for his intervention in their dispute: "Carbide and Carbon Chemical Corporation . . . has ordered a 20 percent cut in wages effective February 4, 1946 for the maintenance lubrication department. Since the reduction is coming in the wake of a 10 percent wage increase given us by the government, approximately 60 days ago, we veterans cannot understand this treatment, as it is certainly evident the present O.P.A. [Office of Price Administration] prices are still too high for us to support our families. We are not unionized, we appeal to you, Mr. President, to intercede in our behalf."

The case involving the Firemen and Oilers is a good example of the tactics unions used at Oak Ridge to press demands even before they were officially recognized. Though they could not go on strike at Oak Ridge, they made their cause known to the president, the NLRB, and the FMCS. Each of these organizations lacked power in the workplace, but the campaign succeeded in forcing the War Department defend its labor policies. This type of bureaucratic harassment helped erode the secrecy around the project and to weaken the War Department's hold over labor relations at Oak Ridge.[30]

Machinists Organize

In the fall of 1945, members of the International Association of Machinists (IAM) also demonstrated that they were longer bound by wartime secrecy rules. The IAM withdrew requests for union representation of machinists at Oak Ridge in August 1945, but in January 1946, it asked to reopen the issue. Defying company and army regulations, the IAM collected cards from 184 of 190 shop employees at the Y-12 plant, including tool and die makers, machinists, blacksmiths, and tool-room clerks. The union also filed petitions to represent workers in the Y-12 experimental machining division.[31]

Both the MED and TEC stonewalled this effort. TEC wrote to the IAM that it could not check the cards against the list of employees because "of the confidential nature of our work" and suggested that elections could not be held "consistently with maintaining the security of this project." Though the IAM failed to win immediate recognition, they were the first group to successfully sign up workers in the plants at Oak Ridge. The act of collecting cards and convincing workers to join the union started to undermine the army's ban on union organizing. Once the MED and contractors began receiving cards and signatures from the IAM, it demonstrated that union organizing was taking place on the shop floor and was not just the work of "outsiders."[32]

Electricians Fight for Representation

The actions of the local union of the International Brotherhood of Electrical Workers helped bring about the recognition of unions at Oak Ridge's plants. The IBEW tenaciously fought the U.S. Army on two issues through the NLRB. First, the union claimed that fifteen of their members had been unfairly dismissed during the war for participating in a wildcat strike. Second, the IBEW pressed for a representation election to be held among electricians at Oak Ridge. By pursuing these claims, and threatening to strike for representation, the IBEW forced the army to agree to hold union representation elections in 1946.[33]

In November 1945, the Oak Ridge IBEW local filed a petition with the NLRB for a union representation election. The NLRB replied on November 15, 1945, that "no action will be taken on the case until such time as Congress enacts legislation relative to the Manhattan Project." But workers at Oak Ridge were no longer willing to abide by wartime rules and agreements. John Oliver, recording secretary of the local IBEW, responded to the NLRB: "We question the legality as well as the propriety of the War Department's position . . . in prohibiting an election, now . . . and that granted that if the War Department did have such extra ordinary rights in time of war, peace having now been declared, such conjectural rights do not now exist. . . . We maintain that an election concerning wage scales could in no way infringe upon the desired secrecy or security involved." IBEW complaints led to further NLRB investigations into the situation at Oak Ridge. On February 5, 1946, Arthur Joy of the NLRB wrote that the IBEW's complaints about workers fired for striking at Oak Ridge were justified: "The strike appears to have been an Unfair Labor Practice Strike." Joy also noted that "the union involved filed with this office a joint petition for certification and that the proceedings were several times postponed and finally cancelled on direct instruction from Washington. As a consequence, the strike really stems from the Board's refusal to proceed with the representation case." He concluded, "We should proceed to enforce the Act unless and until Congress amends the Act to deprive Oak Ridge workers of their rights."[34]

The federal government sought further delay of union elections and recognition. On February 11, 1946, FMCS commissioner Jack Kelly visited Knoxville to meet representatives of the Knoxville Buildings Trades Union, the International Chemical Workers Union and the Plumbers Union to discuss the situation at Oak Ridge. The union representatives told Kelly that they had cooperated fully with the army, and that in return they had received assurances that as soon as the war was over and there was no further need for iron-bound security, the army would have no objection to unions at Oak Ridge.[35]

With no progress forthcoming, the unions gave notice that they would strike at midnight on March 15, 1946. Kelly met with Colonel Nelson at Oak Ridge on February 13, 1946, and asked that a meeting be held in Washington, D.C., to bring the War Department, the unions, and the company together to discuss the situation. Between February 24 and March 1, the army and IBEW met in Washington at the offices of the U.S. Army Corps of Engineers. Kelly wrote that on March 1, the War Department notified the unions that the secretary of war would withdraw its previous request to the NLRB, clearing the way for union representation elections.[36]

This did nothing to clear up the backlog of labor cases in Oak Ridge. On April 18, 1946, NLRB officials Paul Styles and Paul Kuthenau reported to their superiors that the IBEW members fired the previous June were victims of "a gross miscarriage of justice." They concluded that the army had used its power of secrecy to cover up unfair labor practices at Oak Ridge. "The Army's position in this matter is based on a question of 'top-drawer secrecy' or so-called 'security measures,'" they wrote. "The rather sketchy investigation in this case leads me to believe that the army is merely trying to conceal a horrible mess insofar as labor relations on the Clinton Engineer Works are concerned. In my opinion, the Army has been guilty of what almost amounts to a basic suppression of liberties of the workers on the project." Despite union protests, the workers fired for striking in 1945 were never rehired by the company. However, the IBEW, by sticking with their wartime complaints, showed the MED that it would not give up on issues of fair handling of grievances and the need for representation elections. The union even threatened a strike over these issues, though it is doubtful that such an action could have been successfully carried out at Oak Ridge. Local IBEW union officials at Oak Ridge, unpaid and unrecognized, forced the MED to hold representation elections by their tenacity and ability to bring other organizations into the conflict.[37]

The War Department Approves Representation Elections

In March 1946, Patterson decided that workers at Oak Ridge possessed rights to representation and collective bargaining. Patterson wrote to Chairman Paul Herzog of the NLRB, "The War Department now believes that it is possible, consistent with the requirements of national security, to work out procedures under which the NLRB cases which involved the CEW at Knoxville may be handled. This does not mean that the importance of safeguarding the security of this project has in any way diminished, but rather that we now feel that conditions are such that the conduct of elections . . . can take place without endangering that security if certain safeguards are observed."

The War Department would allow elections on one condition: information on how to divide the workforce into bargaining units could be revealed only to the National Labor Relations Board. This would keep workers and unions from knowing the exact composition of the workforce at Oak Ridge. As a "unique group of facilities," Oak Ridge had to be treated differently from other industrial plants, as "under no circumstances can we afford a strike at CEW, and we believe that a skillful handling of representation problems will go a long way towards removing the possibility of such an occurrence." These limits on unions' access to information and right to strike at Oak Ridge facilities would weaken union power from the beginning. Even while the War Department was liberalizing its labor policy at Oak Ridge, it restricted unions' and workers' rights. The department delayed representation elections at other MED sites, telling the NLRB that they should "refrain from affirmative action" in cases of elections at Hanford indefinitely in "the interests of national security." This would leave workers at Hanford unrecognized for two more years. While at Oak Ridge, workers would get a choice of unions through an NLRB election, at Hanford, workers would either remain in AFL construction trade unions or, in the case of production workers, remain unorganized.[38]

The end of the war transformed Oak Ridge beyond recognition. As workers began to think of themselves as permanent residents, they began to demand rights they had not considered important during the war. In both the community and the workplace, Oak Ridge was no longer the fiefdom of the army. This shift was a vital precondition of the union organizing drive of 1946, as it predisposed workers and city residents to questioning military authority and made collective solutions to problems in the community and the workplace appealing.

CHAPTER 7

Postwar Labor Organizing and the Transformation of Community

IN 1946, Oak Ridge resident and anthropologist Thelma Present wrote to her mentor, Margaret Mead, that the city was changing: "There has been a lot of excitement in Oak Ridge since the CIO has started organizing, and we have all been interested in the contest between them and the AFL—and the outcome. . . . I have no doubt that the whole South is waiting to see what happens here. " History proved Thelma Present wrong; union organizing in Oak Ridge was not the first step in transforming the American South. However, the union drives did change the community in ways that no one could have predicted.[1]

After years of army-imposed delay, 1946 was the year the AFL and CIO set out to organize Oak Ridge's production workers. The unions viewed Oak Ridge as a key battleground in the struggle to organize the South, where a vast majority of workers remained non-union despite attempts to win employer recognition though strikes, National Labor Relations Board elections, and National War Labor Board directives. For the duration of World War II, Secretary of War Henry Stimson appealed to the patriotism of the AFL and CIO and asked them to postpone union organizing at Oak Ridge and other Manhattan Project sites. With the close of the war, however, the rhetoric of patriotism became a rallying cry for workers in Oak Ridge to unionize. Using the argument that workers and their families at Oak Ridge had sacrificed to help win the war, workers and their unions pressed the army and its contractors to honor their rights as Americans— the right to unionize, the right to a democratic community and the right to live without restrictions imposed by security officials.

In Oak Ridge, political, social, and economic arguments were intertwined during the organizing drives, and both unions and companies couched their arguments in competing visions of what kinds of citizens workers could become. In Oak Ridge, an enclosed, government-owned-and-operated city, workers and union organizers appealed to workers' sense of patriotism, citizenship, and membership in the community. Since the military and its contractors dominated both the factories and the city, labor organizers took up neighborhood issues and grievances, as well as workplace concerns, to win the support of the workers and the broader community. As workers began to think of the temporary wartime city of Oak Ridge as their home, their consciousness of their own civic status changed. In the union election, they were able to choose which union to support and which rights they wished to pursue. The AFL and CIO, though they had widely different messages in their campaigns at Oak Ridge, addressed the workers in terms of their civil, social, and political rights, as patriotic citizens as well as workers.[2]

Unions at Oak Ridge succeeded in winning NLRB elections at two of the atomic factories and democratized the community. The struggle to unionize in the plants transformed the meaning of citizenship at Oak Ridge. This same type of transformation is also apparent in the findings of Gary Gerstle and Lizabeth Cohen, who discovered in their studies of 1930s Woonsocket, Rhode Island, and Chicago, respectively, that the political struggles over citizenship and government were linked with the economic victories of the CIO. Urban ethnic workers of the 1930s, according to Gerstle and Cohen, exercised their political rights in the streets and in the polling booth at the same time they were organizing their workplaces, using the rhetoric of "Americanism" or "unity" to make demands on both the federal government and their employers. In Oak Ridge in the 1940s, workers mobilized around issues of fairness and lack of political and economic voice, and they demanded their rights as citizens, both in the factories and in their community. Though the results of this postwar drive were not the galvanizing victory that the unions hoped it would be, the city of Oak Ridge and its workers were changed utterly by it.[3]

Oak Ridge stands out in the history of Operation Dixie, the CIO's southern organizing drive, as a modest success in a campaign usually regarded as a complete failure. Historical studies of postwar southern labor organizing have focused primarily on the causes of this defeat and its economic and political consequences. However, this research's focus on failure and defeat neglects the successes, even small ones, like Oak Ridge. In Oak Ridge, the union drives were far from defeated, as labor organized two of three plants at the facility and gave workers the means to fight for seniority rights, higher wages, and pension and health benefits. More important, the union drives helped democratize the city by challenging wartime MED policies that restricted freedom of speech, the press, and assembly. The unions provided workers with a means of exercising citizenship in a community where they could not yet vote for local officials and gave workers a voice as citizens, more than employees living in an Army base.[4]

The U.S. Army's Secret City

Oak Ridge production workers lived in an America without the Wagner Act. Both at work and in the community, Oak Ridgers endured indignities during the war that spurred their organization into unions afterward. In the workplace, the alienated nature of uranium production, arbitrary hiring and firing policies, and the lack of a fair grievance system gave rise to union sentiments. In the community, rising food and living prices, and the powerlessness of living under military and company rule, contributed to unionization. As workers stopped considering Oak Ridge a temporary wartime stopover and began thinking of it as a permanent home, they demanded citizenship rights both in their factories and in the community.

At the end of World War II, workers demanded a guarantee of permanent employment as a reward for their wartime service. Early in 1946, Carbon and Carbide Chemical Corporation and Tennessee Eastman Corporation laid off men and women as part of a "reduction in force," then hired workers at a lower pay rate to take the jobs of those eliminated. The CIO's local newspaper, the *Atomic Worker,* sent an organizer to look for a job at TEC; he was not only offered a job but also told to bring along any relatives in need of work. By August of that year, fifty-nine thousand workers had been laid off in Oak Ridge and twenty thousand hired, making the CIO's case seem plausible to many in the community. At TEC, the number of workers declined from a wartime peak of twenty thousand to eleven thousand in May 1946. The layoffs and lack of seniority protection meant that workers who were thinking of staying indefinitely in Oak Ridge looked to unions to protect their jobs. At the same time, layoffs and quitting at the factories siphoned off many of the temporary-minded workers who were less inclined toward unionism.[5]

Wage rate differentials between workers also made unions attractive. As the CIO told workers, "Men working side by side on the same machines were not getting the same pay. In one building, some workers earned 72 cents an hour and other workers doing comparable work were earning $1.02." The CIO used the slogan "equal pay for equal work" to oppose this company policy and to support female workers' right to equal wages. Workers lacked a fair grievance system. At Carbide, for example, an employee fired for alleged incompetence could go through the company-sponsored grievance system but could not have a representative, or his or her own stenographer, as part of the proceedings. As a last step, the company would choose and appoint an arbitrator to hear the case, but without union or worker input. Even the conservative AFL veteran organizer James Barrett was shocked at what Oak Ridge workers went through. He reported to President William Green of the AFL that "the rotten conditions at Oak Ridge in regard to handling grievances and in termination of employment are so deplorable that one cannot describe the situation by letter. Returned veterans are being terminated and ordered to vacate their houses within a given time, and move families and furnishings from the area." These grievances, especially those involving returned war veterans, gave unions a patriotic card to play in their bid to organize the city.[6]

The military's autocratic rule of the city of Oak Ridge propelled many workers into unions. The lack of a free press at Oak Ridge meant that workers read about the atomic bomb explosion in the *Knoxville News-Sentinel* rather than the military-edited *Oak Ridge Journal*. Civic organizations needed army approval to hold meetings at Oak Ridge. Even local churches needed military permission to hold vestry meetings if they involved more than three people. Unions offered workers a collective voice to press the military for change. As Oak Ridge resident Thelma Present wrote in a 1946 letter, "The people here are beginning to feel that it is about time that they are treated as any other citizens. They want to feel they can ask why, how and where, and have a voice and a right to criticize. Many people honestly believe we have a dictatorship here." Though certainly Oak Ridge was a relatively benign dictatorship compared to wartime Germany or Japan, workers and residents were not inclined to accept any more autocratic rule.[7]

This desire for community freedom and unionism was linked, as the letter of Ophus A. Evans, an Oak Ridge worker and CIO organizer, demonstrates. Evans described what it was like to work in the plants at Oak Ridge to the *Knoxville News-Sentinel:* "The company backs its foremen to the limit. So keep your nose clean and your mouth shut and you will get along." A no-union voter, Evans argued, could "bow down to the 'little Hitlers' if he likes, but I and others like me are for freedom of thought and freedom of expression." Workers at Oak Ridge had labored for the arsenal of democracy during World War II without possessing freedom within their community or their workplace, but with the end of the war, union activists used this combination of patriotism and unionism to appeal to workers who might still be leery of the latter.[8]

The CIO Campaign for Unity and Fairness

The CIO campaign revolved around the grouping of all "50,000 atomic workers into one big effective union." However, this vision initially was blocked by U.S. Army security regulations. The Manhattan Project set the ground rules for organizing: union literature could be distributed only outside plant gates and with prior approval by the army, the army would tell each union when it was permitted to distribute literature, former members of the armed forces would not be allowed to wear their uniforms while distributing literature, and the army reserved the right to terminate distribution of literature at any time for "security reasons." This policy, which was interpreted strictly by military authorities, was so rigid as to make almost all literature distribution illegal. When a union organizer with two boys, ages eleven and thirteen, leafleted at the Carbide and Carbon plant gate, a military policeman asked them to step back from the gate and requested the children's names and addresses. The names were then sent on to the company and to the chief of police.[9]

Army rules made literature distribution virtually a criminal offense in Oak Ridge. At Carbide and Carbon, the army caught AFL and CIO union organizers evading distribution rules. According to official surveillance, an AFL organizer was spotted "within the parking lot of the restricted area. . . . [He] took from his personal car a wrapped bundle of literature, unwrapped some, and distributed some among the automobiles parked nearby and also distributed some to employees nearby . . . in violation of the established procedure in this matter." A worker who supported the CIO was seen "carrying with him a bundle. . . . [He then] went through the post [into the plant area] and proceeded to distribute the literature which he had brought to work. . . . The guard not being sure of his position made no comment and failed to secure the badge number of the employee." Though workers elsewhere in the United States had the right under the Wagner Act to talk union and distribute literature and buttons on their breaks, this was forbidden by Oak Ridge's military authorities. Oak Ridge union meetings also were monitored closely by army and Roane-Anderson police. In fact, police files from 1946 indicate that members of both organizations attended CIO meetings to monitor security violations.[10]

Under these conditions of fear, the task of organizing at Oak Ridge was difficult. Director Paul Christopher of the Tennessee CIO wrote in May 1946 that "the task requires, of course, a legion of volunteer organizers within the plants [425 different buildings at three plants]. We have about 50 [volunteer worker organizers] who are presently doing this Jimmy Higgins work;

later we will have many more." Photographs of Oak Ridge's CIO organizers highlight their youth and optimism, in contrast to the AFL's image as a more established, mature union (figs. 11 and 12). The CIO, barred by the army from having more than a dozen professional labor organizers into Oak Ridge, instead relied on workers to organize each other. Over the course of the campaign, the CIO's position at Oak Ridge strengthened, as these volunteers became the "inside committee" so many Operation Dixie campaigns lacked. Workers could move invisibly within their plant and com-

The youthful staff of the CIO's organizing drive in Oak Ridge, c. 1945. Box 6, Binder 20, RG 434-OR, Still Pictures Branch, NARA.

munity, signing up members, whereas outsiders were more vulnerable to company and army harassment.[11]

The CIO stressed in its campaign that it fought the military on behalf of workers. The CIO paper at Oak Ridge, the *Atomic Worker*, claimed that it had "brought freedom of expression to Oak Ridge" and had given "pitiless publicity to injustices" there, making it "like a fresh ocean breeze blowing after a hot sultry day." Until the union organizing drive began, Oak Ridge had one newspaper, the military-run *Oak Ridge Journal*, which took predictable positions on local issues and was infamous for its time lag

AFL speech in Oak Ridge, c. 1946. Box 6, Binder 20,
RG 434-OR, Still Pictures Branch, NARA.

in news. With the union drive underway in May 1946, the area had the competition of two additional newspapers, the AFL's *Knoxville Labor News* and the CIO's *Atomic Worker*. This expansion of Oak Ridge journalism prompted the federal government to seek a commercial newspaper that would replace the official *Oak Ridge Journal*.[12]

The CIO based its drive on the problems and hardships Oak Ridge workers faced in their community as well as in their workplace. As the CIO's "Oak Ridge Workers' Case" states, "Oak Ridge has been rough living in many respects. . . . [Workers] lived in crowded trailers and tiny rooms for long years. They paid high prices for poor food. They paid higher prices for what little clothing they could be found. . . . They lived—and a great many men are still so living—under substandard conditions which are disgraceful to Oak Ridge and to a country as resourceful as America."[13]

As part of its campaign, the CIO promised to transform the community of Oak Ridge, as well as conditions in the factories. As one pamphlet stated, "In Oak Ridge, the CIO is interested in . . . fair and reasonable standards and criteria for housing allocation; it supports and advocates an adequate housing program for Oak Ridge as speedily as possible; the enforcement of price ceilings and controls; the furthering of health and education programs, for CIO takes a true citizen's interest in the community in which the worker lives. The CIO stands for a socially conscious community. The way to get such a community is to join and belong to a CIO union."[14]

This campaign for the community took several forms. First, the CIO took up complaints about housing in Oak Ridge, channeling wartime frustration with poor service and a low standard of living into the union organizing drive. Rather than treat housing as a peripheral issue, the CIO held up the arbitrary policies of the army and its housing contractor, Roane-Anderson, as examples of how Oak Ridge residents had been denied their civil rights during World War II. Workers' most important complaint was that housing at Oak Ridge was contingent on having a job at one of the plants or contractors. The *Atomic Worker* reported on July 10, 1946, "Once fired, a worker was evicted from his or her place of residence." If TEC were shut down, it continued, "under present regulations in Oak Ridge, the majority of workers would be forced to leave the government reservation and look elsewhere for a home and a job." The CIO pressed to change this policy, and in 1946 it brought a case before the NLRB arguing that if a worker's dismissal was being appealed, eviction should be postponed until a decision had been reached. On July 5 of that year, the *Atomic Worker* reported, "With the help of the CIO, Earl Rodgers, a worker at Carbide and Carbon Chemicals Corp., who was terminated in May, is continuing to occupy his house in Oak Ridge, despite efforts of the Roane-Anderson company to oust him."[15]

However, eviction was only one of Oak Ridge's housing problems. As a July 10, 1946, letter to the *Atomic Worker* shows, the wartime housing crunch had not let up in Oak Ridge: "The housing situation in Oak Ridge has been worrying many people who live in trailers and have been trying for many months to get a house in which to live. Trailers are all right as a temporary measure, but after months and years they get on your nerves." As the wartime emergency ended, workers expected a higher standard of housing, and the CIO used this desire to their advantage, airing worker complaints about housing and pressing the army to build more housing and to rent it at reasonable rates.[16]

Vile cafeteria food was another key issue in Oak Ridge. For workers who lived in trailers or dormitories, Roane-Anderson cafeterias provided the majority of meals. An employee asked the *Atomic Worker* on July 5, 1946, "Can the CIO do anything toward bringing about an improvement in some of our cafeterias in Oak Ridge? . . . Working people who eat at cafeterias need and deserve good, clean food." The CIO took up the cry for better food in its newspaper, exposing the poor service and quality of these establishments. The *Atomic Worker* described Roane-Anderson's food as a sign of disrespect for Oak Ridge's workers:

> Some of the eating places where you charge prices that should burden your consciences, are ill-kept, unclean, sometimes no forks, no spoons or knives. There are no saucers for your cups; no plates for your soggy toast; cold storage eggs; no bacon, no ham; no sausage. They have minced ham, bologna, greasy soggy minced ham, fried minced ham, boiled minced ham, baked minced ham and bologna. As a rule, at many of these places all the food is badly prepared, ill-seasoned, and thrown at workers as though Roane-Anderson were doing the people a great service by allowing them to eat at Roane-Anderson.

Another issue of the *Atomic Worker* contained this description of Roane-Anderson's cafeterias: "bad sanitary conditions in certain eating places and drug stores; the prevalence of flies and other disease bearing insects in public places." These attacks on poor food and service brought home the issue that a year after the end of the war, Oak Ridge's workers were still being treated like army privates.[17]

This community orientation brought both attention and support to the CIO, whose paper received many more letters to the editor about housing, prices, and food than about working conditions and seniority. An editorial in the *Atomic Worker* linked the community freedom brought by the

CIO with the job security promised by the union: "What will it profit a man to be able to vote for his representatives in government if on the following morning he receives an eviction notice from his house? How much consolation for him to be told that he is a free American citizen, if after long, patient toll on his job, he is terminated to make way for a less experienced person willing to work for 50 cents less per hour?"[18]

To win these workplace and community benefits, the CIO argued, would take a strong and unified labor union. As part of its goal of unity, the CIO targeted the votes of women workers during the campaign with the slogan "Equal pay for equal work." In a pamphlet titled *The Woman and Her Job*, the CIO pointed out that women's wages were 25 percent below men's wages at one Oak Ridge plant. "Is the woman worker an economic old shoe, to be used only in the war emergency or at the lowest wage rate, and to be cast aside at the whim of the employer?" it asked. The organization promised female workers that "it is the CIO's policy and practice to establish equal pay for equal work, with no discrimination as to sex." It also promised women "participation in industrial democracy in a CIO union" where "women and men stand shoulder to shoulder in the common cause," concluding, "In the CIO women workers are finding the way to better wages, better working conditions, and to real economic equality based upon no discrimination." The *Atomic Worker* exposed poor working conditions at TEC, where a female employee wrote that chemical operators "are not allowed to even go to the washroom and wash the poisonous chemicals from our hands before dressing." After each shift, "the worker checks out dripping with perspiration and hands sore and dirty from strong chemicals. It's a shame that such things exist in a free country." The CIO promised that a union contract would give women a chance to wash up, on company time, before leaving each shift. The CIO also hired a professional organizers, Esther Demeo, to organize women at TEC, where the majority of women worked, and sought the votes of women who worked at K-25 and X-10 as well. Since women workers at Oak Ridge had seniority, and had not replaced men to get their jobs, they were in a better position to keep their jobs after the war. This made women's votes vital for the CIO, and their concerns could not be ignored.[19]

The union also hired a full-time organizer to work with African American workers at Oak Ridge, as they had the lowest-paying, hardest jobs, as well as the worst housing conditions. Promises of higher wages and better treatment were welcome in the African American community, whose members predominantly held maintenance positions in the plants. The AFL had been unresponsive to the job concerns of African Americans in

Oak Ridge during the war. Job discrimination claims filed with the President's Committee on Fair Employment Practices by African American carpenters against Knoxville AFL unions show that they had been unwilling to deal fairly with African American skilled workers.[20]

The *Atomic Worker* also sought to align workers with scientists on the project, indicating contact between the two major occupational groups at the facility. Scientists and engineers in Oak Ridge had their own organizations, which united and became the Oak Ridge Association of Engineers and Scientists, affiliated with the Federation of American Scientists. The scientists' groups were not labor unions but instead promoted civilian control of atomic energy and world government. The *Atomic Worker* newspaper featured articles on scientists at Oak Ridge, including "Army Case Built by Attack on Scientists," which charged that the House Un-American Activities Committee was a dupe of the army, trying to maintain military control over atomic weapons. The *Atomic Worker* also published laudatory articles on the scientists' movement, such as "Scientists Today Speak as Group: Gets World's Ear." However, this attention and coverage was not reciprocated—materials from the Association of Scientists and Engineers contain no mention of workers or the CIO. The scientists and engineers' organizations also explicitly excluded workers from membership, insisting on a college degree for membership.[21]

The AFL Campaign

Unlike the CIO, the AFL began its campaign in Oak Ridge with a longer track record in the region. The AFL represented construction workers in Oak Ridge, many of whom remained after the completion of the plants to work in production or skilled trades jobs. Machinists, firemen and oilers, and electricians in Oak Ridge had been agitating for over a year before the army permitted union organizing. Machinists at Y-12 had petitioned the NLRB for an election to join the International Association of Machinists, as did the Firemen and Oilers International Brotherhood. The IBEW at Oak Ridge, which included both electricians working construction and those working inside the plants, had been the most militant during the war, going on a brief wildcat strike to try to force recognition of their union at the K-25 powerhouse. However, the military at Oak Ridge squelched these early AFL efforts. The army requested the NLRB not to act on the AFL petitions during the war, and the electricians at K-25 were fired and evicted from their houses for their illegal strike. This conflict left a bitter taste in the mouth of Oak Ridge craft unionists, who felt betrayed by both the army and the contractors.[22]

The AFL campaign at Oak Ridge revolved around the theme of Americanism. The AFL's Oak Ridge radio broadcast opened with James Barrett, its Oak Ridge organizer, telling the audience, "My country, 'tis of thee! Wonder how many of us are giving thought to the welfare of our country." The broadcast ended with the song "God Bless America." AFL publications assured workers who had never been part of a union that the AFL, and unions in general, were an American tradition. In the AFL's *Knoxville Labor News*, Oak Ridge edition, the AFL relayed that "Oak Ridge workers, coming from school room and farm at the call of their country have had little opportunity to learn of vote procedure in National Labor Relations Board Elections." The AFL assured workers that it and the NLRB were "American," not subversive institutions. Claiming that it embodied America, the group was "more typically American than all national groups. The historic mission of the American Federation of Labor is to spread prosperity. There is no place in AFL for Communists, PAC or similar front groups; It is Deep Rooted in the American Soul." This implied that the CIO, with its political action committees and northern accents, could not claim the same.[23]

The AFL's Americanism had two faces—one reassuring workers, one attacking the CIO. The AFL appealed to worker conservatism by stressing that "the American Federation of Labor is a staunch supporter of states' rights," "home rule," and "self-government in your organization." It pursued two goals with this hyperpatriotic rhetoric: first to discredit the CIO, second to convince rural workers with little union experience to trust the AFL's brand of Americanism. AFL literature charged that Charles Doyle, an officer in the CIO's Chemical Workers Union, was a Communist and asked, "Has anybody here seen Doyle—Communist Member of CIO Board?" Tennessee state AFL president John Hand told workers that "no Reds from Niagara Falls will have any control over Oak Ridge local unions if they are AFL."[24]

As part of this theme of Americanism, the AFL attacked military and company rule of Oak Ridge. The union refused to submit its periodicals for predistribution review by the military, and in July 1946 the military dropped this requirement for union literature. The AFL also attacked General Groves as an overrated, publicity-seeking fraud. An issue of the *Knoxville Labor News* told readers, "General Groves [is] not so hot here in the Atomic City," as scientists and workers, not military men, had built the atomic bomb. In July 1946, outraged with security regulations that limited their organizing drive, the Atomic Trades and Labor Council of the AFL released a letter comparing Oak Ridge to a dictatorship with Groves as its "Lord and Master." The AFL charged that the army violated "every principle of the four freedoms and every concept of a free government." According to the union, even conquered Japanese workers had more rights than those in America: "While General MacArthur has prepared and is putting into operation in Japan a plan of freedom, the Generals in command of Oak Ridge, in the United States of America, have destroyed freedom and established a dictatorship as hateful as any Hitler brand of dictatorship. MacArthur has issued a decree that labor in Japan must be free to organize their Trade and Labor Unions; Army officials here at Oak Ridge block every efforts by Americans to form unions."[25]

Like the CIO, the AFL campaigned for the votes of women workers on the grounds that it had supported equal pay for equal work and an end to wage differentials between male and female workers. In an appeal to female laborers, the AFL advertised that it had ended the seventy-two-hour week for women in manufacturing establishments and claimed that workers "now enjoy the forty hour week with price and one half for overtime; all because of the long, hard struggle made by the AFL." However, citizenship had its limits in the AFL campaign, as seen in the drive for women workers' votes. The AFL promised help in the workplace for women if needed but voiced its preference that women remain at home. One AFL flier reminded men in regard to the upcoming NLRB election, "You be the judge—You are head of your own household. You have to be the judge of what is best for your own family." The AFL pamphlet *Women in Industry and in the Home* shows that the AFL was more comfortable appealing to family values than to woman workers: "Many men have died that women might have better lives." Further, it declared that "industry gradually shackled American womanhood to the machine, doing so for the sole purpose of reducing wages and increasing profits." In fact, the AFL seemed almost schizophrenic in its treatment of women on the job. On the one hand, it offered them equal pay, on the other, it suggested they return to the home.[26]

The AFL had no such divided consciousness when it came to the rights of men, who were portrayed as heads of their households in union literature. When Carbide and Carbon Corporation sent a letter to workers urging them to ask their families about the election, the AFL replied in an open letter to plant manager Clark Center, "Don't you think that I am capable of making my own decisions without consulting my dependents? If I were not, would I have the right to call myself 'breadwinner' or 'provider' for my family?" Clearly, the AFL defined itself as a male union, with an image of both providing for a family and making the decisions for that family.[27]

Yet the AFL recognized the need for women's votes in the NLRB elections and appealed to them as potential AFL members. "These women [at

Oak Ridge factories] are not free," the AFL wrote in one press release. "Any one of them can be terminated at the will or whim of the boss. They have no job security, no seniority rights, no grievance procedure, no voice in anything pertaining to their working conditions, wages, hours, or conditions of employment." The sheer number of women working at Oak Ridge (more than four thousand at TEC alone) meant that they could not be ignored in union elections, forcing the AFL into a more liberal position on matters of working women than it otherwise might have taken. In radio advertisements, however, the ideal AFL member was clearly male. As one script noted, the "welfare of women and their children has been the inspiring purpose of the labor movement since its very inception. The wage-earner has ever looked at his pay envelope with the bare-faced fact imprinted upon his mind that it contained everything his wife and children would be able to enjoy."[28]

Racial lines also defined citizenship for the AFL. The union would only go so far as to sponsor a party for African American workers before the election, and it never mentioned African Americans in campaign literature. The AFL never apologized or distanced itself from AFL building trades' discrimination against blacks during the war. The campaign did remain free of racial slurs or divisions, for fear that any votes lost in the election could spell total defeat for the AFL, but internal memos show that the union saw itself as representing the "Anglo-Saxon citizens of the hills of Tennessee."[29]

Despite the AFL's rhetoric of unity, its unions struggled among themselves throughout the campaign. AFL officials fought a long, losing battle to force its coalition of trade unions to present a unified voice in Oak Ridge. Unlike the CIO, the AFL Atomic Trades and Labor Council was comprised of independent unions that often worked at cross-purposes. While AFL organizer James Barrett sought to present a united front, he had no authority to order changes in local union policy. For instance, Barrett publicly denied that the AFL unions were charging unreasonable initiation fees at Oak Ridge. However, in letters to AFL Southern Organizing Drive director George Googe, Barrett wrote that several AFL unions at Oak Ridge, such as the Painters and Decorators and Sheet Metal Workers, were continuing their policies of "high initiation fees and broken promises." Barrett charged that this "created a chaotic condition" in the AFL campaign and this lack of coordination "created [a situation] that we fear . . . will cause us to lose the elections in at least Tennessee Eastman and Carbon-Carbide." If workers believed that the AFL would not stand united, Barrett argued, why would workers cast their ballot for the union?[30]

Divisions between Knoxville and Oak Ridge AFL members also hindered the organizing drive. Barrett charged that Knoxville Building Trades union leaders were in "fear that workers at Oak Ridge . . . will overthrow the Knoxville group and demand jurisdiction over all Oak Ridge work. The Knoxville boys express the sentiment that inasmuch as they put up the money for the campaign, they should now have control over the work and the men. The Oak Ridge boys counter this argument with the assertion that Knoxville unions have collected untold hundreds of thousands of dollars off Oak Ridge workers in initiation fees, dues, fines assessments and issuances of permits." This lack of unity between unions, and between Knoxville and Oak Ridge workers, only hurt the AFL in its campaign, turning workers off to the AFL's brand of decentralized unionism.[31]

Disunity within the AFL was a common problem in its organizing efforts nationwide. In the AFL, workers belonged to a union of their trade, but those unions were free to pursue their interests, even when these came into conflict with other AFL trade unions. Unlike the CIO, which promised unity, AFL unions pledged that smaller, autonomous unions within an AFL framework would represent workers. This gave the AFL unions a more exclusionary definition of citizenship in which those outside a craft, or women or African Americans, had less of a claim to the economic and political rights of Americans. However, attempting to appeal to a large, heterogeneous workforce in Oak Ridge, the AFL did not make trade, skill, race, and gender divisions central to its campaign, instead focusing on the defects of the CIO and misdeeds of the military.

The Companies' Anti-Union Campaign

The contractors at Oak Ridge had their own definition of good citizenship. They portrayed themselves as rational, benevolent employers and the unions as unnecessary intrusions into a fair and just employment relationship. Although less public in their efforts than the unions, the companies at Oak Ridge, particularly Tennessee Eastman, tried to convince their workers to vote for "no union." Their strategy is detailed in a series of memos to managers at the three plants, memos that found their way to the files of James Barrett. Tennessee Eastman told its supervisors to remind workers of TEC's commitment to "a policy of fair play and 'the square deal'" and to "keep before the employees, for their full comprehension, evidences of the employee benefits they now receive: Vacation, Life Insurance policies, Wage dividends, Working conditions (clean, well-ventilated, comfortable, no excessive hours, etc.), Freedom of discussion." TEC also attempted to rebut charges that it laid off employees only to hire new workers to take their place at lower wages. "We don't discharge people arbitrarily," it claimed. "When a reduction in force is necessary, the employees affected by it are first ranked, not just according to seniority, as the unions would have it, but according to performance, length of service, and attendance. . . . New hires have been less than one half the number of employees that have voluntarily resigned since V-E day." Under strict NLRB guidelines, TEC sought ways to make plant management seem like a reasonable and fair collection of men and the two unions appear hotheaded and full of promises they could not deliver. The companies' arguments hearkened back to welfare capitalism, in which the company portrayed itself as a democratic institution, responsive to worker complaints.[32]

The NLRB Elections

Photographs of the August 1946 NLRB elections are striking in several respects (fig. 13). First, lines of workers, black and white, men and women, lined up before and after work to cast their ballots. For many blacks from the South, and for poor whites who could not afford the poll tax, the act of voting was a belated confirmation of their citizenship at Oak Ridge. More than 90 percent of workers cast ballots in the NLRB elections held on August 21, 1946. The results of round one were that in all three elections, a runoff was needed, since in no case did the CIO or AFL, or the category "No Union," win a majority of votes (see table).[33]

The election results disappointed the CIO leadership but did not cause despair. Operation Dixie director Van Bittner telegraphed his organizers, "Tell the boys not to worry about the results of the election at Oak Ridge. I know you all did everything humanly possible and that's the best anyone can do. Keep your chin up." The CIO explained its poor showing to workers of Oak Ridge by noting that the "CIO has been in Oak Ridge about three months. Other unions have been in Oak Ridge for more than three years." The *Atomic Worker* continued to press for victory at Carbide and

Number of Votes in NLRB Round One Elections at Oak Ridge

Company	CIO	AFL	No Union
Tennessee Eastman	1,531	1,721	2,579
Monsanto	121	289	176
Carbide and Carbon	1,429	1,612	1,373

Oak Ridge's first free election, NLRB balloting, August 1946. Box 6,
Binder 20, RG 434-OR, Still Pictures Branch, NARA

Carbon and Monsanto in the runoff. It told workers, "Organize—CIO victory is within the grasp of every CIO member and worker in Carbide and Monsanto." The CIO urged TEC workers to vote "No Union" so that the CIO could petition for another election if the AFL failed to win a majority of votes. The CIO also promised a $1.00 initiation fee (free to veterans) and maximum dues of $1.50 per month, unlike AFL's high initiation fees (sometimes over $100.00) in addition to dues and assessments. Finally, the CIO promised one union for all production workers, and it raised the possibility that production workers could be split into many different unions under the AFL, including the "hod carriers and common laborers international union." It asked workers, "Can you afford to be classified as a hod carrier or laborer?" For many workers, the title "hod carrier" was meaningless or demeaning, making the AFL system of breaking the plant workforce into separate unions seem outdated. The CIO also represented a step up for unskilled workers in the plants, as a CIO victory would make all Oak

Ridge workers equal in one union, reducing the importance of the line between skilled and unskilled workers.[34]

Following this inconclusive election, the NLRB scheduled a second round of balloting for September 10-12, 1946. Under NLRB regulations, if "No Union" was in second place in the balloting but one other union received 20 percent of the vote, "No Union" would not appear on the runoff ballot. The second round of NLRB elections split the Oak Ridge workforce three ways. Monsanto, the smallest employer, voted for the AFL by a two-to-one margin. At Carbide, the CIO won by the slim margin of 1,918 to 1,893. At TEC, "No Union" won, 3,120 to 2,503. In all three elections, turnout exceeded 70 percent, with 88 percent of workers voting at Carbide and 91 percent at TEC.

Several factors account for the split results of this election. Carbide's K-25 plant was closest in structure to the industrial plants of the Northeast and Midwest, which the CIO had previously organized. Many of its chemical process workers were former coal miners with union experience in CIO founder John Lewis's United Mine Workers. Monsanto's X-10 plant was smaller in size, with a large contingent of machinists and skilled workers, giving the AFL a solid base of support not found at K-25.

Tennessee Eastman's Y-12 plant voted No Union for several possible reasons. First, Y-12 suffered the most from layoffs, with the workforce declining from more than twenty thousand to thirteen thousand between September 1945 and January 1946, giving a temporary quality to its operations. TEC was also the most openly paternalistic of the companies and had the most women working in the facility, many of whom saw themselves as temporary workers. Even so, in the first round of NLRB elections, more than 50 percent of the workers there voted for a union, with the vote so evenly divided between the AFL and CIO that No Union won a plurality. The shortsighted decision of the CIO to ask its members to vote No Union in the second round accounts for the union loss at that plant.[35]

Events the night of the election marred any hope for cooperation between the newly created AFL and CIO locals. The AFL challenged the vote count at Carbide, claiming that ballots had been improperly filled out, though the NLRB did not uphold this challenge. AFL leaders charged the NLRB and CIO with cheating and vilified the contractors and the army. When a Mr. Crawford of the CIO told AFL leader James Stewart, "Congratulations on Monsanto, tough luck on the other two," Stewart responded, "Yes, thanks to you, and give the Colonel my thanks. We'll get you s.o.b.'s yet." The situation only got more tense during the recount that night, when AFL leaders, described by the MED reports as "drunk—a fact which made their charges more reckless and also increased the possibility of violence," charged that the NLRB had fixed the election. The ballots were escorted to the train station in a police radio car and put on the midnight train to Washington for safekeeping. The NLRB summoned the military police, and the ballot counting ended without violence. However, the stage was set for bitter resentment between the unions rather than unity against common foes.[36]

The union drives at Oak Ridge resulted in a split decision, as the AFL, CIO, and "No Union" won one plant each. This split left unionists in Oak Ridge frustrated, and both the AFL and CIO would try in the next few years to win the other two plants. Cooperation between the two unions was out of the question as a result of this competition and the bitterness that remained after the organizing campaigns were over. As negotiations began with Carbide and Carbon Chemicals and with Monsanto, the union movement at Oak Ridge was divided, rife with suspicion and jealousy. Nevertheless, the situation at Oak Ridge was far better for union workers than at the Hanford, Washington, production facility, where the Atomic Energy Commission did not allow workers to organize or bargain collectively until 1949.[37]

Unions made a powerful impact in Oak Ridge. While many Operation Dixie campaigns left only bitter memories in their wake, unions and the rights unions won for residents of the community became a permanent part of Oak Ridge. Freedom of the press, the right to distribute literature in public, the right to criticize the military, and the right to join a union were established by unions' organizing drives. When the fence that surrounded the city of Oak Ridge finally came down in 1949, it was a legacy of the union campaigns to open the city to the outside world.

CHAPTER 8

Victory in the Community, Stalemate at the Bargaining Table: Unions, 1947–1954

FOR AMERICAN LABOR, 1946 was a year of crisis. Workers and their unions pressed a long list of demands left unresolved during World War II: raises to compensate for wartime inflation, input over corporate decisions, health insurance, and health and safety policies. The United Automobile Workers (UAW), United Steel Workers, United Mine Workers and United Electrical Workers all struck that year, and their actions reverberated throughout the nation and the federal government. Settlement of these strikes set the course for postwar bargaining, as the unions made wage and benefit gains but were unable to make a dent in the "managerial prerogatives" that companies held to manage their workforce. Congress, dominated by Republicans and southern Democrats, began in 1946 to legislate restraints on the power of unions to strike. It attempted to bar strikes in many industries, including facilities necessary for defense needs or the "health and safety" of the nation.[1]

In Oak Ridge, the victory of production unions in National Labor Relations Board elections did not lead to the promised sweeping changes in the production plants. Instead, the CIO and AFL victories were the beginning of a long, frustrating process of bargaining between unions and contractors over wages, seniority, and working conditions. Oak Ridge unions, through collective bargaining, sought guarantees that the wartime promises that brought them to the city would be honored. They looked for guarantees that high wages and the availability of work, housing, and community services would continue at Oak Ridge, even with the end of the wartime emergency. Further, workers and their unions demanded a greater voice in the workplace, particularly over health and safety issues. However, the contractors and the federal government had other goals. Government contractors sought to standardize Oak Ridge's employment system with other chemical plants nationwide, eroding wartime benefits and wage differentials. Both the contractors and AEC resisted worker attempts to influence safety policy, insisting that work in the plants was safer than at other chemical plants and that the companies and government should maintain full control over production.[2]

The Liberals Turn against Labor
DAVID LILIENTHAL

No one person was more important to the development of Oak Ridge's postwar labor policy than AEC chairman David Lilienthal, a most unlikely antagonist for the city's unions and workers. When President Truman nominated Lilienthal, then chairman of the Tennessee Valley Authority, for the job as chair of the new AEC, organized labor overwhelmingly applauded. When his nomination was attacked in the Senate, CIO president Philip Murray wrote, "The CIO and the American people as a whole are convinced that on any basis of justice, decency or ability to handle the job, Mr. Lilienthal should be confirmed speedily for this new assignment." This advocacy was based on Lilienthal's role in TVA and his image as a progressive.[3]

At the outset of his career, Lilienthal had supported the rights of workers. In his diary entry of December 24, 1919, Lilienthal, then age twenty, wrote, "My greatest interest now, as before, has been in Labor; largely, I believe, because it has so close a human connection. . . . My interest in industrial conditions and means of ameliorating its undesirable features; my indignation at the inequalities of distribution of wealth, causing a surplus at one extreme and insufficiency for the common decency on the other, has been of relatively long standing." His concern for workers motivated Lilienthal to become a lawyer who would represent workers and consumers against the corporate giants that ignored their interests.[4]

Lilienthal's indignation did not last through his tenure at TVA. There, he became disillusioned with labor unions, especially the AFL craft unions with which he worked closely. "A closed shop removes the necessity for labor officials to stir their bones and do a job for their membership," he wrote. "They become dues collectors. They become just as fat-headed and sterile as they dare to be . . . and a closed shop in a tight industry gives the opportunity for about the maximum of inertia and fat-headedness."[5]

Other political forces moved Lilienthal and the entire AEC to the right as well. Lilienthal was forewarned that his work at AEC would be closely watched for signs of radicalism. During his contentious AEC confirmation, Tennessee's Senator McKeller and other congressional conservatives had savagely attacked Lilienthal for being too soft on communism and other security risks while at TVA. Unlike the TVA, Congress and President Truman expected the AEC to work closely with corporations in the field. The AEC would not be a "yardstick" to force private companies to provide better service to the public for less money, as TVA had been, but a cheerleader for and a midwife to the atomic energy industry.

In the postwar years, Lilienthal steadily drifted away from labor unions and toward the corporations he had challenged earlier in his career. His outlook shifted to a pro-business and pro-enterprise stance, especially when it came to the development of atomic energy. In a speech to Oak Ridge union members in 1948, he declared, "The Commission certainly believes that this atomic industry can never flourish and grow and find its proper place among the elements of our national strength unless it sends its roots deep and wide into the same soil that has nourished the automotive and other industrial giants, the soil of competitive private industry. . . . We do not forget that the mammoth developments inherited from the Manhattan Project were built, improved and operated by American industry under governmental direction." Lilienthal's shift from a pro-labor to pro-corporate position is a prime example of the shift many New Deal liberals made. In Lilienthal's case, it would have a profound effect at Oak Ridge, as unionists there had been counting on him being on their side.[6]

First Postwar Labor Negotiations

Fearing a flood of returning soldiers saturating the labor market, in 1946, Oak Ridge's workers and unions sought to guarantee their future employment. This would come at a price, however. The CIO's United Gas Coke and Chemical Workers (CIO-UGCCW) was told in October 1946 that any contract with Carbide would include a clause that made any "stoppage or slowdown" a cause for immediate dismissal. This ban on strikes left the union without recourse in case of disputes. The union also had to agree that the "continuity of operations" would take precedence over any other issue in labor relations. As a result, no matter what the status of negotiations were, work at the plants would continue.[7]

On December 10, Carbide and the CIO announced that the agreement was complete. Though the pay increase was substantial (ten cents per hour), postwar inflation threatened to erode it quickly. The lack of provisions for sick time, holiday pay, and vacation pay meant that workers would be on the job continuously or take unpaid time off. This contract was disappointing compared to other unions' 1946 victories. In Detroit, the United Automobile Workers were attempting to "open the books" of General Motors to link wage raises of thirty cents per hour to corporate profits. After a short strike, the UAW settled for a raise of eighteen and a half cents per hour. John L. Lewis's United Mine Workers negotiated a health and welfare fund to pay retirement and health benefits for workers and their families. The first UGCCW contract was, by these contemporary standards, anemic.

The AFL's first contract benefited from bargaining with Monsanto after the Carbide and Carbon negotiations concluded. Monsanto had taken over control of the X-10 plant on July 1, 1945, from the University of Chicago, which had run the plant since 1943. This fragmentation of management favored the union in negotiations, as the current management team only had been in place for little over a year. The union negotiated with Monsanto from November to mid-December and agreed to a contract with the company on December 17, 1946. This contract included craft wage rates between $1.605 and $1.785 per hour, a victory for the AFL in comparison to the results of the Carbide/CIO negotiations. The AFL's higher base wages made Monsanto workers the highest paid workers in Oak Ridge, well above their fellow workers at Carbide and Carbon and Tennessee Eastman. When the terms of the AFL contract was announced, the CIO charged that Monsanto had been too favorable to the AFL.[8]

A Chill in Labor Policy

While the AFL and CIO fought over who had received the better deal, the AEC stewed over the results of negotiations, regarding both contracts as giveaways. In January 1947, the commission asked labor experts Lloyd Garrison, David Morse, and George Taylor to read over the Oak Ridge contracts and suggest changes. These three men, liberals by reputation on questions of labor relations, found the contracts too lenient toward the unions. They warned that the two contracts provided for different wage and benefit levels, which could lead to "'whip-lashing' under which each union will try to gain for itself advantages previously obtained by the other, and then to seek further gains on top of that." They recommended amending the AEC policy to limit access to any classified information and permit firing of any workers suspected of subversion. In the climate of the early cold war, even liberals such as Garrison found that the government had a right to fire those it suspected of subversion without a hearing or trial, though he would argue otherwise only a few years later, when these policies were applied to top scientists such as J. Robert Oppenheimer.[9]

With the onset of the cold war, Oak Ridge once again moved toward the frenetic activity that had dominated the facility during World War II. The threat posed by a new enemy, the Soviet Union, served as a powerful means to reactivate the patriotic consensus that had dominated Oak Ridge during World War II. The enemy had changed, the language had shifted to a "cold war" and "containment," but at Oak Ridge, the message was unmistakable: the facility would be back to full production as it had during World War II.

The AEC used the cold war emergency as an opportunity to tighten security procedures that had been relatively lax during World War II. Plant employees violating relatively minor work rules (such as being absent several times without an excuse) might face a full security review. These investigations would include full background checks. If prior criminal convictions were found, the employee could be dismissed. Unions perceived these investigations as witch hunts, as they often involved union officers or employees simply guilty of bad luck. In one case, an African American janitor was charged with being a security risk. Even though the man was cleared by the local security advisory board, the AEC Oak Ridge manager overruled the board and fired the employee.

In another case, a union officer was attacked as a security risk. A union member who attended the security "advisory board" described it as follows: "The 'Board' sits with a file, presumably compiled by the FBI, and stated 'we have been informed' of this or that, but the 'board' cannot be compelled to produce those making these accusations. Neither can the accused have any access to these records. Actually, it amounts to a kangaroo court of the worst sought, and is completely void of any resemblance of the democratic rights supposed to be every American's."[10] However, security proceedings such as this continued, and evidence of prior criminal convictions, talking to outsiders, or asking the wrong questions could lead to a man or woman losing a job without appeal.

New Issues of Health and Safety

In the context of tightening AEC labor policy, Oak Ridge unions found it more difficult to negotiate contracts with their employers. There were two reasons for these problems. First, Congress and the AEC viewed all labor actions at Oak Ridge as a threat to national security. Second, the unions and workers began raising issues of health and safety in these negotiations, topics that the AEC and contractors wanted to keep off the table and out of the newspapers. The contractors might have seemed an easy target for unions, as they were able to pass along increased personnel costs to the federal government. However, contractors fought to keep wages in line with the rates for their other facilities, and they sought to prove their toughness to the AEC in order to keep their contracts. The AEC itself organized its contractors, bringing them together to discuss future wages, contract negotiations, and the maximum "limits beyond which they should not go without giving us notice."[11]

While the AEC and contractors could view higher wages as an acceptable price to pay for labor peace, neither would tolerate union interference with health and safety issues in the plants. On August 19, 1947, the CIO issued a message to members on health and safety describing the union's frustrated effort to set up a joint health and safety committee. The union also prepared a resolution on health and safety, calling for a "joint committee to investigate the dangers of employment at Carbide, and to give every Carbide employee a thorough examination." The AEC asked the CIO to discontinue issuing these resolutions to the press, as they "contradict the AEC official news bulletin."[12]

On September 1, 1947, the CIO held a bargaining unit meeting for members to hear about the Carbide Corporation's latest offer. Three hundred employees met at the CIO union hall and were told that thirty-one union requests had been turned down by the company, which instead proposed six items for worker concessions. The workers unanimously rejected the company's offer and instead allocated five thousand dollars to send a committee to Washington, D.C., to "discuss health, safety, lack of good faith in bargaining . . . with the AEC, the JCAE [Joint Congressional Committee on Atomic Energy] and the President." The union planned a motorcade to Washington, loaded with petitions from workers for better wages and working conditions. During the union meeting, an AEC observer noted, "several voices suggested that the employees 'go fishing'" and absent themselves from their jobs rather than submit to Carbide's conditions.[13]

In order to bring pressure on their employers and the AEC, on September 2, the CIO organized "Oak Ridge's First Labor Day Celebration." At noon, a parade of cars and trucks, all bearing CIO signs, marched from the union hall through the town to the picnic area. The parade was two miles long and featured color guards from the Veterans of Foreign Wars and American Legion. Speakers at the rally included National Organizing Director Van Bittner of the CIO, President Martin Wagner of the UGCCW, and Director Paul Christopher of the Tennessee CIO, as well as Representative

Estes Kefauver, who, the AEC recorded in its labor diary, "is much more violent in his denunciation of Taft-Hartley than any of the union men."[14]

On September 11, 1947, the CIO released a statement asking, "Why should Carbide get so upset when the Union requested an impartial investigation in respect to health conditions at Carbide after the death of Wilton Rhodes Earle? If health and safety conditions at the plant were proper, why should Carbide hesitate to endorse an impartial investigation?" Earle, who had worked at Carbide and Carbon in 1945 and 1946, died in Austin, Texas, in August 1947, and his autopsy revealed radioactivity in his liver.[15]

With negotiations stalled, the federal government and media considered the strike a potential threat to national security. The Federal Mediation and Conciliation Service, the agency responsible for assisting with labor negotiations, began preparing papers on December 6 that would allow President Truman to invoke the emergency "cooling-off period" in the Taft-Hartley Act to stop a strike at Oak Ridge. When the United Gas, Coke and Chemical Workers of Oak Ridge held a strike vote in March 1947, *New York Times* headlines proclaimed, "Strike Vote Perils U.S. Atomic Output." The Atomic Energy Commission told the *Times* that it should be "obvious to everyone that interruption of production is unthinkable." The rhetoric of impending crisis, coming from both the government and the media, made workers appear selfish and unpatriotic for exercising their right to strike and took pressure off the company and the AEC to negotiate a settlement. Nevertheless, the UGCCW went back to the negotiating table with Carbide and Carbon, and on December 11 at 5:00 A.M., a settlement was reached.[16]

X-10 and Taft-Hartley

On the heels of the tense dispute between Carbide and Carbon and the CIO, the AFL began negotiating its new contract at X-10. The plant was now run by the same contractor, Carbide and Carbon, that ran K-25 and Y-12. An AFL stronghold, X-10 paid the highest wages of any of the area plants. In the new negotiations, the AFL had promised its members further gains, while Carbide and Carbon sought to lower pay and benefits at the plant to the level of other Oak Ridge facilities. When the AEC asked Carbide and Carbon to take over the management of X-10, workers at the plant immediately realized that the company would attempt to bring wage levels at X-10 down to the level of Y-12 and K-25. The AFL craft unions at X-10 protested to Lilienthal on January 15, 1948: "We are deeply concerned over and in opposition to the proposed change in Clinton National Laboratory. . . . We feel that it creates an unhealthy condition for Labor if one company should gain control of all the operating plants in Oak Ridge engaged in Atomic Energy work. This would tend to give them a monopolistic hold on work being done here as well as on the workers doing it."[17]

Workers at X-10 feared that Carbide and Carbon would reduce wages, eliminate their ninety days of unpaid sick leave, and stop providing safety and protective equipment and clothing free of charge. Carbide and Carbon took the approach that X-10 workers should receive the same wages and benefits as other company workers: less pay, fewer benefits, and no free protective equipment and clothing. The company also wished to end the liberal disability policy for X-10, substituting a shorter period of disability with less pay. A presidentially appointed fact-finding board accepted company figures about accidents and ruled that though there was a great "potential hazard" from radiation at X-10, the "effective hazard" was much less than elsewhere in the chemical industry. The board concluded, "Despite the favorable accident experience of the past, the Union maintains that X-10 workers are apprehensive because they realize the potential hazard which is unseen and mysterious and because they doubt the ability or willingness of the new contractor to maintain the safeguards of the past. In spite of these apprehensions, the record of labor-turnover and the measures of difficulty in obtaining workers presented to us by the AEC indicate that, by test of their conduct, workers are not averse to employment at X-10."[18]

The union raised the question of safety equipment in the X-10 negotiations. The Presidential Fact Finding Board appointed by President Truman to study the dispute noted that "the Union contends that employment in the laboratory entails greater hazard than in the other two plants" and that "work at the Laboratory exposes its members to potential hazards of unknown kind and degree." The company sought to have sole authority in determining which equipment was needed, while the union sought a joint (worker-management) safety committee to make this determination.[19]

Union demands for health and safety protection continued. The union also sought "indemnification" for the future health effects of radiation. It wanted to "indemnify all employees of the U.S. AEC from any ill effects of radiation or contamination for the rest of their natural lives. If it becomes scientific or medical fact that their descendants will likewise suffer injurious effects, the descendants will be indemnified also." This would "bind the contractors to pay for all future ill-effects of radiation even to future generations." The company maintained that this was outside the scope of contract negotiations and the proposal was dropped.[20]

As negotiations dragged, the health and safety issue began to make its way into press reports. Reporter Victor Reisel of the *New York Post* visited

Oak Ridge in March 1948 and found workers "furious enough to quit working at X-10." Not only was the dispute over wages a factor in the strike, but Reisel found workers angry about working conditions and sick leave policies. He wrote that the work at Oak Ridge was "dangerous," that the "mystery of unseen radioactive waves add terror" to the job. Workers, he noted, "wear little danger meters [dosimeters]—some round, some like pencils—on their shirt pockets or coat lapels and the doctors make the rounds regularly to keep men from collapsing as the invisible rays eat into the blood cells. Just before that the men turn listless and lethargic, act like robots."[21]

The demand for sick leave, Reisel wrote, was justified, as "some of [the workers] need the rest. Collapses are frequent and X-10 men don't die. They are weakened by radioactivity . . . and [are] highly susceptible to the common cold, pneumonia, influenza, and other viruses floating about at the moment. The X-10 experimental workers suddenly grow dull and move mechanically and need two days rest to tone them up again." This sickness had even affected union negotiations, as "one [union] committee member collapsed in Washington while waiting to meet Mr. Truman's belated special Conciliation Board. The atomic worker, weakened by work at X-10 and the trip up to the capital, had to be taken back to Oak Ridge by car."[22]

According to Reisel, the company's desire to "restrict issuance of protective clothing" was a major stumbling block in negotiations, as was the difference between the wage increase the union sought (fifteen cents per hour) and the increase the company offered (eight cents per hour). Reisel chided the company and the AEC for being "silly" as the "Government and the Atomic Energy Commission hasn't had the sense to look down and see that the mighty atom is split by the hands of working people, who scare like the rest of us, and have as high a cost of living as the rest of us."[23]

After a month of failure in negotiations, President Truman invoked the Taft-Hartley emergency provisions at X-10, forbidding any strikes, lockouts, change of practices, or change of employment status on the part of the union or the company. Federal District Judge George Taylor heard the case for an injunction, which would enjoin AFL from "encouraging, causing or engaging in a strike, . . . or in any manner interfering with or affecting the orderly continuance of work" at Oak Ridge and bar the Carbide and Carbon Chemicals Corporation from "making any changes in the wages, terms and conditions of employment."[24]

This action infuriated both the AFL leadership and its rank and file. Workers at X-10 who wrote to the JCAE were angry with the Truman administration, the AEC, and Carbide. James Weber, an Oak Ridge worker, wrote to the JCAE, "While you are making a law forbidding a man's right to strike, how about making one giving him the same rights that other Americans enjoy? The class segregation on housing is enough to get any one disgusted with Oak Ridge. Have you examined the labor turnover at Oak Ridge? How do you think this situation affects the security of the project? I have been here less than one year and do not intend to stay much longer and in view of the present situation here, would hardly recommend anyone else coming here. I would like to see the Joint Committee look into the housing situation."[25]

This sentiment was shared by other AFL workers at Oak Ridge. On June 8, 1948, a mass meeting of X-10 workers gathered to denounce Lilienthal and the other AEC commissioners. The resolution read:

> Whereas the workers at X-10 (ORNL) do hereby go on record as opposing David Lilienthal for any reconfirmation as chairman of the AEC because of his open support to a vicious contractor in our lengthy labor dispute. Lilienthal's statement that if the X-10 workers strike the commission would order Carbide to operate the laboratory shows clearly that he is no longer the worker's friend. We further condemn him for his implied strike-breaking tactics. Therefore be it resolved that we respectfully request our various international unions and the public to oppose Mr. Lilienthal and his fellow commissioners reconfirmation to the AEC, as being too small in stature to assume and carry out the vast responsibilities necessary to protect our national interest and welfare.[26]

By 1948, the union's struggle for higher wages and better working conditions had resulted in a stalemate. However, the stalemate was not just between workers and corporations but also between workers and the federal government. The AEC and its contractors were able to keep raises in hourly wages down during this period—34 cents per hour total (to $1.60) between 1946 and 1949, a time period when inflation rose 10 percent nationwide. While these bread-and-butter gains were substantial, they represented only a fraction of the wage rise of industrialized workers, such as those in automotive fields.[27]

Union Action on Housing and Civil Rights

While Oak Ridge's unions, both the AFL and CIO, struggled to gain improvements in wages and benefits, they also took a role in community development. The AEC and the contractors frustrated unions' attempts to win concessions, but in the community, unions found influence and the power to force the AEC to concede on several important policy issues. In the areas of housing policy and civil rights, unions in Oak Ridge were able to challenge the AEC effectively, in part because these conflicts were out in the open, public realm, as opposed to the secretive closed world of the plants.

In 1949, Oak Ridge unions spearheaded the drive to head off a rent increase proposed by the AEC. They launched a petition drive that garnered six thousand signatures of Oak Ridge residents demanding a congressional investigation of AEC management of rental housing in the city. Together with the town council, the unions asked that Congress investigate waste and mismanagement in the AEC housing program. The union accused the commission of failing to properly maintain Oak Ridge's housing stock, leaving workers in unsafe and unattractive living quarters. The AEC's housing policies had baffled and frustrated residents for years. These policies included a prohibition on workers moving from nearby communities to Oak Ridge, excessive charges for cleaning and maintenance of rental units, and even reclassifying renters as "licensees" whose Oak Ridge housing license could be revoked at will by the AEC. In spite of the unions' efforts, the AEC rejected the union's drive against rent increases and imposed the higher rents on May 15, 1949.[28]

The rent issue continued to aggravate workers. In 1951, when the AEC requested a 28 percent rent increase for Oak Ridge housing, the local CIO union pursued the issue on a national as well as local level. At the behest of the CIO, Estes Kefauver, now a U.S. senator, introduced legislation to establish a rent board for Oak Ridge to approve AEC rent proposals. United Gas, Coke and Chemical Workers of America president Martin Wagner petitioned both the AEC and Congress for action on Oak Ridge workers' behalf. This pressure orchestrated by the union forced the AEC to postpone the rent increase and to begin to investigate selling Oak Ridge's housing stock to workers.[29]

Even after this rent increase failed, unions continued to push for lower rents in the city. In August 1951, Jerry George, who served both as an official of the CIO local in Oak Ridge and on the advisory town council, requested that the secretary of defense place Oak Ridge under a system of rent control as it was a critical defense area with a housing shortage. In October, the issue was tried in county court, where the AEC argued that housing was adequate in the city. George argued that the AEC had increased employment in Oak Ridge by five thousand workers while cutting the number of available housing units by five hundred. The court, in a rebuke to the AEC, ruled that the area had a housing shortage, and in December 1951, rent stabilization began in Oak Ridge, making the AEC powerless to impose rent increases on city residents.[30]

Although rent stabilization came to an end with the inauguration of the Eisenhower administration two years later, Oak Ridge unions continued to press the AEC for a fair deal in selling housing to workers. Several officers of the union set up a housing cooperative to help workers buy houses from the AEC once they became available. Unlike the issues of control of the workplace, or plant health and safety, unions had real success in fighting against AEC community policies. They built a coalition of civic leaders, local newspapers, and local and federal officeholders who joined together to fight, and on occasion defeat, AEC policies.

Oak Ridge unionists also were involved in the fight to desegregate Oak Ridge's school system. In 1953, members of the Oak Ridge town council asked the AEC to "end segregation in Oak Ridge schools." In Oak Ridge, the AEC could desegregate schooling in the city at will, as there was no local or state authority to oppose the move within the federal reservation. Almost immediately, however, local opposition to this motion arose. The AEC simply refused to act on or answer the request. In February 1954, Waldo Cohn, chair of the town council, faced a recall vote based on his opposition to segregation. The AFL and CIO both supported the council and argued that segregationists were dividing the community and distracting the city from real issues, such as rent increases. On February 9, voters in Oak Ridge narrowly defeated the segregationist challenge, the recall vote failing to gain the needed two-thirds majority by only 250 votes out of more than 5,000 cast. An advisory committee on desegregating the schools, headed by Oak Ridge scientist Karl Morgan, also suggested immediate desegregation to the AEC, which did not respond.[31]

When Oak Ridge schools were desegregated in January 1955 as a result of the *Brown v. Board of Education* decision, there was no violence in the city, while in neighboring Clinton, desegregation provoked riots and a bombing at the high school. The Clinton crisis became national news when New Jersey native John Casper, head of the White Seaboard Citizens Council, led whites in resistance to the enrollment of blacks at the local high school. In Oak Ridge, a powerful federal presence and strong local institutions could restrain even die-hard segregationists, while in Clinton, segregationists were able to capitalize on local grievances to provoke a crisis that required the intervention of the Tennessee National Guard.[32]

While the fight over desegregation was supported by unions in the city, the status of African Americans within these unions was not clear. A 1960 report by Elizabeth Peele into employment policies at Oak Ridge found evidence of employment discrimination by craft unions, noting that "very few Negroes [were] employed above low-skilled or janitorial level." While the unions' record of fighting for a desegregated Oak Ridge community is extensive, their ability to create integrated unions was less than exemplary.[33]

Unions in Oak Ridge exerted far more influence within the community than at the bargaining table. Union leadership, in both the AFL and CIO, took the lead in many community issues, including rent stabilization and school desegregation. These efforts—aided by the national unions, Tennessee politicians, and community leaders—brought about rent control in Oak Ridge and helped force the AEC to address local school segregation.

CHAPTER 9

Postwar Occupational Health and Safety Problems

1131 building was, as I described, quite frankly a hell-hole.
—WORKER TESTIMONY TO DAVID MICHAELS, DOE ASSISTANT
SECRETARY OF ENERGY FOR ENVIRONMENT, SAFETY, AND HEALTH, 1999

OLIN SMITH was a stubborn man. In May 1946, Smith, a member of the Planning Department at Ford, Bacon and Davis, filed suit in federal court against Carbide and Carbon for injuries to his throat and vocal chords. He believed that working on an unventilated, fume-filled "cleaning platform" caused a series of serious throat ailments, culminating in the loss of his voice. Smith wrote, "This area consisted of about thirteen tanks, most of which contained alkalis and acids for removing rust, smut, etc. . . . When pipe was submerged in tanks and left for several minutes and brought out again great clouds of steam were given off. This vapor, of course, included alkalis and acids [and] . . . were very unpleasant and irritating to the nose and throat."[1]

Smith found the ventilation in the entire area to be inadequate. "I had often wondered about the ventilation system since the time someone poured a chemical into the wrong tank, this was a small area located only a few feet from where I worked," he noted. "The chemical reaction created a dark brown rope of smoke some four feet in diameter that rolled across an open area . . . and across receiving area towards offices . . . where it broke up. . . . Apparently, there was no exhaust or method of removing clouds of vapor from the cleaning area." Smith went on leave, then came back to work briefly for Carbon and Carbide inspecting valves at K-25. However, the fumes from this second job forced him to leave once again, this time for good. He sought help from doctors to diagnose his condition but received only vague diagnoses such as "chronic laryngitis."[2]

Smith, unlike other accident claimants, filed suit against Carbon and Carbide. He told the court, "I seek damages because I have suffered a great loss. I do not think I have to go into detail about what one loses when he loses the facility of speech. There are many things one loses." Smith's case would never be heard in court. After a delay of more than five years, in 1952, the AEC refused to release information about Smith's workplace as it was "restricted data"; an AEC memo detailing why the information was restricted was not available to the court. U.S. District Judge Robert Taylor retired the case from the docket until information became available, thereby leaving the matter in legal limbo.[3]

AEC documents about the case, released decades later, show that Smith was correct in his suspicion that his workplace was ill-ventilated. In a meeting of the Occupational Disease Claims Advisory Board, Carbon and Carbide denied the accusation, claiming, "the only possibility of exposure to the claimant would be from . . . oil which has a chlorine base. He had suffered no damage from any such exposure." However, further investigation revealed that "the claimant might have been exposed to trichlorothylene fumes, [and] arechlor oil fumes which may have been contaminated with a residue of uranium salts from process and silicon and magnesium dust or asbestos dust." The shop in which the man worked was poorly ventilated, and an industrial hygiene report covering this period noted that the area was contaminated with arechlor (oil), fluorocarbons, and trichlorothylene. Though the AEC still would not admit that these substances caused Smith's lung condition, a member of the medical section noted, "Inhalation of fumes by a patient with asthma often markedly aggravates his condition."[4]

The AEC Occupational Disease Claims Advisory Board suggested settling with Smith, as "it would be practically impossible to defend this case since the facts show a violation of the Tennessee Statute of Ventilation." The highest settlement the AEC was prepared to make was three thousand dollars. Yet a settlement between the AEC and Smith never was reached. Neither the AEC nor Carbide and Carbon ever paid him a cent.[5]

Smith's case raises important issues about Oak Ridge's occupational safety. First, it exposes the barriers Oak Ridge workers faced in proving that an injury was caused by their job, when so many of the employment conditions were a national security secret. Second, his case demonstrates how even when the AEC recognized its possible guilt, it refused to publicly admit any fault or damage. Finally, Smith's case is remarkable in his steadfast fight to win compensation—how many other cases were simply dropped upon initial refusal to pay compensation? The documentary record of Oak Ridge's facilities, while incomplete, reveals many cases in which, in the postwar period, workplace safety was given a lower priority than the speed of atomic materials production.

The Cold War and Safety

Safety problems at Oak Ridge did not disappear at the end of World War II. Instead, the growing cold war put Oak Ridge's atomic materials production back on full throttle. New processes, needed to build an arsenal of atomic and hydrogen bombs, required a retooling of Oak Ridge's production facilities, and these new processes brought new hazards. The cold war sent Oak Ridge back toward the frenetic activity that had dominated the facility during World War II. As one Y-12 worker recalled, "We felt that we were under a timetable—a seven day a week, 24-hour a day time schedule. . . . When this [the cold war] started, we were in a race to develop a hydrogen weapon." This new emergency helped create new hazardous conditions for workers at Oak Ridge and institutionalized many already existing hazards.[6]

The avoidance of responsibility for worker and community health problems is not unique to the AEC. As many recent histories of occupational health and safety have demonstrated, many employers in hazardous industries have shown little concern for workers' well-being. Instead, illnesses such as silicosis and lead poisoning, and cases of toxic chemical exposure, have provoked industry efforts to evade legal responsibility for harm. With the power to classify documents at will, the AEC could fend off challenges by unions and workers with ease.[7]

Classifying Evidence of Danger

The Manhattan Project classified scientific evidence, produced by MED scientists, that radiation and radioactive substances caused cancer. In March 1946, the MED Public Relations Office halted declassification of three scientific manuscripts produced at Oak Ridge by government scientists on radiation and cancer. These papers, which included "Induction Tumors in Rats with Beta Rays From P32" and "Carcinogenic Effects of Fast Neutrons and Gamma Rays on the Lungs of Mice," demonstrated that a single high-level dose of radiation could lead to skin and subcutaneous cancer, with rats dying two to three months after exposure. When the MED handed over Oak Ridge to the AEC in 1947, the documents remained under wraps.[8]

The newly created AEC used their authority to limit access to information about radiation dangers and human experimentation. In May 1947, the AEC Medical Section stated that a similar paper on inhalation of fissionable materials and fission products should remain classified because "plutonium and fission products are at present controlled and handled by the AEC installations only, . . . [and] the withholding of this report will not materially affect the outcome of any outside research." The AEC also suggested that "at least one human experimentation case is discussed in the latter part of this document, and because of medico-legal reasons, it is deemed inadvisable at this time to release this information." This reference to "medico-legal reasons" demonstrates that the fear of being sued made publishing the results of studies on the biology of cancer improbable.[9]

The postwar era actually saw a reduction in material available to the public about the dangers of radiation. In 1947, the AEC began reclassifying work that had previously been declassified, finding new reasons to impose security restrictions on the publication of AEC cancer research. Papers on the "Distribution and Excretion of Plutonium" and "Uranium Excretion Studies" were found to "involve matters that might be prejudicial to the best interests of the Atomic Energy Commission." The broad, unregulated use of the power to classify allowed the AEC to keep its problems and mistakes out of the public eye. Classification protected these government agencies from scrutiny and lawsuits, leaving workers and citizens without recourse or even knowledge of government policy.[10]

The Postwar Era at K-25

Problems in K-25, particularly in an area called "the cascade," only intensified after the war, giving it a reputation among both workers and managers as a particularly hazardous building. A K-25 worker who began work at the plant in 1951 recalled, "In the early days of using 1131 building, A-feed building, . . . it was probably the worst conditions I have ever worked in, in any building anywhere. Not just in any Oak Ridge, but other workplaces I have been. Conditions were extremely difficult, intolerable, totally unacceptable then and would be today." The system to prevent and monitor workplace exposure to radiation and chemicals was inadequate for the building. "In those days," the worker continued, "and particularly in the 1950s and 1960s, formal training was practically an unheard of item. Workplace monitoring and safety [were] very sparse and very scarce. . . . The rad[iation] protection was totally inadequate then." This testimony indicates that in the postwar period, there was little departure from wartime practice. Even as scientists and physicians better understood health and safety standards and issues, practices in the plants at Oak Ridge did not substantially improve.[11]

Another person who worked in the same building during the 1950s confirmed this description of the building: "I admire the folks that brought up 1131 because that was a punishment place. I was sent to in 1952 when it started up. We dealt with uranium, it was a feed and tails plant actually. We produced the uranium from UO_3 to UO_2 to UF_4 and from UF_4 to UF_6 and fed it into the cascade to be enriched. The UO_3 came in from Hanford, Washington and Savannah River, South Carolina, which they told us would not have any plutonium in it, but I found out that anything that came from Hanford or Savannah River reactors did contain plutonium."[12]

Though there was plutonium and other hazardous chemicals used in the building, monitoring was primitive. A K-25 worker recalled, "We wore film badges and every time they would get a little bit hot they would bring me into the office and say you have deliberately contaminated that badge. You put it in the ash receiver and left it overnight. Also after that they got to showing up hot so often they gave us condoms to put over the film badges." Even lunch brought no relief from radiation and other chemical hazards. As the canteen was in the building across the street from the cascade, dust could escape and enter the eating and drinking area. As one worker recalled, "We had a window air conditioner [in the canteen] that was not putting out any cool air, just sitting there humming and we got to complaining about it. They sent maintenance people over to pull the outside off and looked and it was completely plugged up with UF_6. And they ran us out and we had to eat outside for a few days while they decontaminated the lunch room and replaced the air conditioner." This exposure, as it occurred at lunch, would not necessarily be monitored and recorded in an employee's permanent record, underestimating exposure to workplace hazards.[13]

A third former K-25 worker and manager testified that in the early 1950s, despite some efforts to create a safe workplace, the hazards in the building simply overwhelmed available resources. He testified that his "assignments subjected personnel to various hazardous conditions associated with raw uranium, hydrochloric acid, fluorine and mercury, which I have helped flush down the floor drains per instruction of the supervisors." Despite working with high levels of hazards, this worker reported that few safety procedures were in place: "I worked with a very poor knowledge of the associated hazards and under a weak monitoring system, resulting in exposure and injury to me and my coworkers. We were assigned industrial hygienists who would monitor equipment and attempt to limit our work time in exposed areas. But these guidelines were suspended if manpower was not available for our immediate release."[14]

Though much more needs to be known about workplaces at Oak Ridge such as K-25's Building 1131, the evidence uncovered thus far indicate that far from being an improvement, the 1950s and the Korean crisis led to an increase in occupational health and safety problems in the plants.

Y-12 in the Postwar Years

A plant with a dismal safety record during World War II, Y-12 continued its track record of problems into the postwar era. Air quality at Y-12 did not improve, and safety inspectors declared areas of the plant unsafe even to workers who wore a respirator. In February 1946, a TEC worker was severely injured in a gas-poisoning incident, despite wearing a GI gas mask on the job. TEC officials noted that the mask was properly used and in good condition, indicating "comparatively heavy concentrations" of toxic gas in the atmosphere. Safety officials also complained that employees of Building 9202 had come to accept the presence of toxins in the atmosphere as normal. However, there were not enough gas masks to distribute at TEC to workers in need of them, as they were on order with suppliers.[15]

Poor safety practices at Y-12 had a cost, and workers who labored in the chemical recovery section paid the price. A sample of worker complaints about conditions at Y-12 filed from 1945 to 1947 reveal that the product recovery areas were a continual source of accidents, injuries, and compensation claims. Complaints of occupational injury were denied or passed on to TEC's insurance company for payment. In one case, TEC internally admitted culpability for an occupational injury but publicly fought the accusation. After occupational injury claims were settled, there is no evidence that TEC or the federal government carried out follow-up studies or examinations. Instead, with the plant shutdown in 1947, injured workers were terminated with the rest of the workforce and allowed to scatter, taking with them medical evidence of the plant's hazards.

As a result of poor document storage and disposition practices, the total number of injuries at Y-12 will never be known. An incomplete set of injury and accident reports released by the Oak Ridge Operating Office provide some information about health and safety at Y-12. For instance, these records (fifty-five in number) show that twenty-four injuries occurred in the areas devoted to uranium recovery, Departments 185 and 186. Eleven workers were overcome by fumes and suffered lung problems as a result. Seven more accidents were caused by acid leaks or splashes, as part of the process in which metal parts would be placed in tanks of acid to remove uranium residue. If representative, these records provide a cross-section of injuries at the plant and indicate that many of the hazards of the plant were concentrated in a few departments.

The Chemical Division, which included Departments 185 and 186, employed a maximum of fifteen hundred employees at the facility at any one time, out of more than ten thousand total production employees. If representative, numbers suggest that a division with less than 15 percent of the plant's workers generated 43 percent of its accident claims. This staggering proportion was a result of the philosophy of the Chemical Division, which sought to increase production of uranium, even if it meant high employee turnover owing to health issues.[16]

TEC ignored injuries that should have served as a warning sign. Project scientists knew that the presence of dermatitis, an inflammation and discoloration of the skin, was an indication that hazardous chemicals or radiation were in contact with a worker's skin. Radium dial workers in the 1910s and 1920s developed similar symptoms, and TEC should have initiated an investigation when its workers developed skin problems. Yet the men and women with these dermatitis cases were treated with coal tar and sent back to work. In 1946, one male worker stated that he thought "dust or something has caused dermatitis to appear on the back of [his] legs and abdomen." He was sent back to work after being examined by a Y-12 nurse. Another female worker in Department 185 developed the condition on both arms, which developed into carbuncles in the afflicted areas. The AEC certified that this was a case of "occupational disease that arose out of and in the course of . . . employment [at TEC], and her disability was due to said occupational disease." This admission, however, was not made to the woman injured, but to TEC, so that their insurance company could reimburse them for the disability payments. These dermatitis cases were not followed up in any systematic way by TEC or the AEC, leaving unanswered the question of long-term effects of exposure to Manhattan Project chemicals and radiation.[17]

The product recovery areas of Departments 185 and 186 continued to send workers to the infirmary with lung problems. A thirty-five-year-old female recovery operator reported "since she breathed fumes and metallic dust in recovery process her chest has hurt." She was treated by TEC physicians and at the Oak Ridge Hospital but was kept on the job and given oxygen treatments. A chemical operator in Department 185 was sent for a checkup after nitric acid fumes escaped and spread throughout the department. A thirty-year-old white female chemical operator in Department 186 was referred to TEC Medical when she was scrubbing parts and inhaled some of the fluid used in recovery operations. She was treated with bed rest, oxygen, and medication, then returned to the line after missing one day of work. A white female chemical operator who "[took] a gasket off [a] dissolver to drain it, and got a whiff of gas" while wearing a mask was treated for "tightness in chest, slight cough, sore throat." There is no evidence in the records that the conditions that caused these problems in Departments 185 and 186 were ever addressed.[18]

Acids burned workers, both the production workers who monitored the machines and the maintenance workers sent to fix mechanical problems. In September 1945, a twenty-one-year-old man reported being burned when an unidentified liquid sprayed on him in TEC. The liquid was never identified by TEC, and the man simply was treated for burns and sent back to work. A white female worker, age forty-two, was burned on her right thumb from washing parts with acid at TEC and was terminated the next day. Another chemical operator, a thirty-four-year-old woman, was burned with acid that "sprayed out from [an] acid hose on [the] left side [of her] face, [her] right arm, left leg, left shoulder and center breast." She returned to work after three weeks. A twenty-one-year-old female was treated for acid burns after "steam in stills was turned on, [and the] stills started spurting acid on her right arms and neck." She returned to work the next day. An equipment cleaner was working with $KCr_2 O_7/ H_2So_4$, and reported a sore throat that lasted for thirteen days as a result of fume inhalation. A TEC official defended safety practice in this case and wrote, "This procedure of cleaning equipment has been in effect since the date this laboratory has been in operation, and to my knowledge there have been no complaints of fumes from same." TEC never admitted to the problems caused by the use of acids in its Y-12 plant and the human cost of using acids to salvage uranium from machinery.[19]

This partial record contains cases that could have served as a serious warning of health hazards to plant officials, had they been properly investigated and acted upon. In August 1945, when a fifteen-hour lapse in ventilation from Department 185 caused twelve workers to complain of lung irritation, TEC investigated the background of the workers to learn whether there was "an industrial background which might predispose these employees to special susceptibility." TEC could find no such common factor and concluded, "The . . . hazard in Building 9206 requires extensive revision, both of the equipment and the ventilation system." The monthly safety report included a discussion of a lower "severity rate" for the month, a result of fewer lost-time accidents, as the workers injured in Building 9206 did not miss work as a result of their exposure. This system of keeping statistics, based on whether workers missed their assigned shift, downplayed chronic exposures and long-term injuries and allowed TEC to believe that it was not harming workers.[20]

If at all possible, TEC kept cases out of court by not telling workers that they had been exposed to radiation. One such worker, a woman at Tennessee Eastman from 1943 to 1945, cleaned equipment to recover uranium, which was "warm" (radioactive) and emitted "uranium, and HCl [hydrochloric acid] and Cl [chlorine] fumes." Project officials noted that the woman suffered from nephritis (kidney failure) and declared, "It appears with some degree of probability that the disease was occasioned by exposure." This woman, as of 1945, was "unaware of her condition, which now shows up on routine physical check and analysis." Her case was considered to be only the first of many to come: "Medical officers anticipate that we will have continued cases of this character." Those affected would suffer "permanent impairment of kidney functions." Out of fear that such actions would lead to litigation, TEC did not track these problems.[21]

Some Y-12 workers turned to Congress to collect compensation. Paul Hudson Hood, a former Y-12 employee, sued Tennessee Eastman, and when his case was caught in the federal court system, he requested his congressman introduce a private bill for his relief. Hood, by then living in New Mexico, asked for twenty thousand dollars to pay for tuberculosis caused by the "deadly nature of the dangerous gases, materials, dust, fumes and poisonous particles and elements which he was ordered and directed to handle, work among and come in contact with." In addition, Hood alleged that "he was not instructed how to protect himself" by TEC, leaving him permanently disabled. He claimed that the AEC and TEC refused to allow material to be admitted in court about the dangers of Y-12, a charge David Lilienthal denied to Congress. The private bill died in the Judiciary Committee of the House of Representatives at Lilienthal's request.[22]

Health problems linked to employment at TEC were not always recognized by workers until after they had left Oak Ridge. A woman who worked as a chemical operator wrote to TEC after the end of the war to ask whether her employment there might have led to her present health problems:

> Since leaving Y-12,… I have been afflicted with a chronic illness, which has almost caused me to lose my life. The illness which was caused from working with the chemicals or acids of which my work consisted of, probably from inhaling the fumes that erupted from the reactors over which I worked, seem to be permanent and may yet cause my death. Records at the Y-12 area hospital will show that I was treated there for severe headaches. These headaches occurred more frequently and three weeks after my termination with your company. I was confined to bed.

Like the other cases discussed above, this incident was not investigated. At the end of TEC's contract in Oak Ridge in 1947, the company turned over its records to the federal government and moved out of Oak Ridge. The records of the health problems left behind in the wake of TEC's health and safety records were simply boxed up and placed in storage.[23]

The "Rattlesnake Handling Cult"

The lack of attention to safety at Oak Ridge did not go unnoticed by other safety professionals. H. M. Parker, Hanford's chief medical official and a member of the AEC's Safety and Industrial Health Advisory Board, found in 1948 that the wartime attitude toward safety had not changed. "A faith method of operation, indigenous to Tennessee, was detected in many hazard problems," he wrote in regard to safety at Oak Ridge. "When questioned about certain hazard procedures, the answer was, 'I believe that it is safe.' The answer was given in cases that other observers currently consider hazardous, and in other cases where experimental verification was possible but was never attempted. We deduce that this is an intellectual version of the less-hazardous rattlesnake-handling cult also indigenous to the region." Unfortunately, this faith was not enough to create a safe workplace in Oak Ridge, and it was workers who paid the price for this method of operation.[24]

CHAPTER 10

The Reckoning: Long-term Health and Environmental Effects

AS AMERICANS CELEBRATED the dropping of the atomic bomb on Hiroshima, the long-term effects of radiation were not yet a concern. Shortly after the end of World War II, scientists within and outside the federal government began to address the issue of radiation's damage to both humans and the environment. Among the first to weigh in publicly was Indiana University geneticist Hermann J. Muller, author of the groundbreaking 1927 research on genetic damage due to radiation. His research showed that there was no dose of radiation that did not cause some genetic damage, though this damage might not be immediately recognized.

Muller's research led him to oppose any large-scale human exposure to radiation, even in low doses. In 1946, he wrote an article for *American Weekly* entitled "Time Bombing our Descendants" in which he argued, "Every atomic bomb probably injures and kills more people in the future than of the time when it explodes. Its radiation is planting in today's survivors millions of those germinal time bombs for posterity to reap. And even the peacetime employment of atomic energy, and, for that matter, x-rays, will bear these fruits if we do not guard their use with utmost rigor." This warning about the effects of the bomb went unnoticed at the time, as the long-term effects of radiation seemed less pressing than the threat of immediate destruction described in John Hersey's *Hiroshima*.[1]

Muller persisted in his protest of radiation exposure. In his 1950 article "Some Present Problems in the Genetic Effects of Radiation," he wrote, "I believe that it is very probable . . . [that] long term effects [such as] lowering of the length of life [are caused by] . . . the cumulative action of many small doses of radiation." These changes, he added, "would not be revealed by the usual blood counts, still less by such signs as the falling out of hair. . . . They are very insidious, elusive effects, gotten at only statistically, yet produced by doses much lower than we thought." Muller's criticism called into question the entire AEC safety program, which was based on blood counts and film badges and did not investigate effects below the threshold of exposure considered safe.[2]

The AEC responded to criticism by independent scientists by denying that radiation caused long-term health effects, classifying information on the subject, and sponsoring studies designed to show the relative harmlessness of working at facilities such as Oak Ridge. (The AEC also sponsored Muller's radiation research during this period.) Throughout the 1940s, the MED and AEC classified documents that showed health risks from radiation or revealed that the government had conducted human radiation experiments.

For the AEC, the best defense was a strong offense. In the 1950s, the commission sponsored the first epidemiological research about worker and community health at Oak Ridge. AEC scientist Jack Moshman wrote a report about cancer rates at Oak Ridge to clear up the "great deal of speculation concerning the hazards of employment, or residence, in the 'atomic city.'" His study claimed that "cancer incidence in Oak Ridge appears to be significantly lower than the national rate," adjusted for age, about half that of the general population. He computed an Oak Ridge rate of 123 cancer cases per 100,000 people, versus a national rate of 260 per 100,000.[3]

The AEC studies did not end scientific criticism of radiation policies. Following up on Muller's work, scientists raised a number of concerns about AEC safety policy during the 1950s. Spurred on by the debate over nuclear testing and fallout, scientists outside AEC turned their lens to the health effects of radiation. Oxford University's Alice Stewart investigated the effects of pelvic x-rays on pregnant women and their fetuses and found an increase in the rate of leukemia in the children whose mothers had received pelvic x-rays during pregnancy. This study was the first to suggest that doses of radiation thought to be "safe" were, in fact, a health risk. Congressional investigations of uranium mining revealed this AEC-subsidized industry was highly dangerous to workers because of the constant inhalation of radioactive gasses.[4]

In the 1960s, two public health experts challenged the view that low levels of radiation were harmless. Ernest Sternglass of the University of Pittsburgh began investigating the effects of nuclear fallout on young children in upstate New York, where high fallout levels had been detected in the wake of U.S. nuclear testing. Sternglass followed Alice Stewart's hypothesis that low doses of radiation could cause leukemia and found that children born in years with maximum fallout faced a higher likelihood of developing that disease. In an attempt to deflect mounting scientific criticism, the AEC hired Thomas Mancuso, a professor of Occupational Health at the University of Pittsburgh, to measure the effects of radiation on worker mortality. Mancuso, finding the records of exposure at Oak Ridge too fragmentary to work with, instead chose to investigate workers at the Hanford facility. Using Social Security data, Mancuso matched nuclear workers' mortality with that of their siblings. He compared the death rates and age of death, finding that atomic workers were dying younger than their counterparts. This finding did not point a finger at any one workplace hazard; instead, it showed that the combination of hazards in the workplace negatively impacted worker health.[5]

Government epidemiologists and health physicists declared Mancuso's method unsound. However, Mancuso, when his AEC contract ended, continued his work in this area, writing several follow-up studies of worker health at Hanford. Collaborating with Alice Stewart and George Kneale, he examined the link between radiation exposure and cancer at Hanford. Their work showed an excessive number of brain, lymphatic, kidney, lung, pancreatic, mouth, and liver cancers for those exposed to radiation in their work at Hanford. In 1979, John Gofman, a former AEC researcher, followed up on this research and argued that exposure to even low, "permissible" levels of radiation caused an increase in the cancer rate of workers at Hanford.[6]

The AEC and its successor, the Department of Energy, funded epidemiological research by in-house researchers to disprove these studies. This research found that death rates for nuclear workers were lower than for the general population, but that in each study, some excess of the expected amount of cancer was found, consistent with prior research on the effects of radiation on human tissue.[7] However, in 1992, Physicians for Social Responsibility (PSR), a group of antinuclear physicians, released *Dead Reckoning*, a report detailing the shortcomings of DOE's epidemiology program. The document concluded that the federal government's atomic workers epidemiology program "is seriously flawed, inadequate in scope and pace of work, under-funded in relation to the studies that are needed, and burdened by the intrinsic conflict of interest and public's recognition of that conflict." PSR also noted:

> Secrecy has plagued the entire . . . operation and is totally inappropriate in investigations of health and safety. . . . The virtual monopoly held by DOE-sponsored researchers on the raw, epidemiological data . . . has been harmful to science, to the principle of open and unfettered research, and to the more rapid and comprehensive explorations of the effects of low level radiation. . . . The findings of the DOE-sponsored studies offer

no firm basis for the repeatedly expressed official position that the health of workers and the public has been fully protected and that there are no excess risks of disease and death in the nuclear cohorts.

The group demanded that DOE open its records to outside researchers in order to let scientists outside the DOE system use the data for independent health studies.[8]

In response to outside challenges to its epidemiology program, the DOE opened researcher access to original data files of many studies and hired university researchers to independently study the issue. Several studies at the University of North Carolina's School of Public Health at Chapel Hill showed elevated cancer and mortality rates for workers in Oak Ridge.[9] Using publicly available cancer rate data, public health researcher Joseph Mangano analyzed the cancer rates in Tennessee around Oak Ridge and compared them to similar rural areas in the Southeast, as well as to the national cancer rate. He found that the cancer rate in Oak Ridge for whites increased 34 percent between 1950 and 1987, compared to 5 percent for the nation. In the non-urban counties near Oak Ridge, where cancer deaths should be lower, this rate increased 39 percent, versus 23 percent for urban areas near Oak Ridge. Cancer death rates grew faster in mountains surrounding the facility, rather than in the lowlands, and they were higher downwind of the facility than upwind. These findings suggested a negative impact on public health by AEC activities in the Oak Ridge area.[10]

Community Health and the Environment

The hazards of the atomic production process did not end at the plant gate. The radiation and chemicals used in Oak Ridge's production facilities affected the entire community and surrounding environment. The legacy of atomic weapons production at Oak Ridge will outlast the generation of workers as well. Workers handled hazardous materials inside the plant, which then were released into the air, land, and water to become a community health risk. Radioactive materials do not disappear into the environment—many have a half-life of centuries. Despite this, even less is known about the impact of Oak Ridge's waste on the local community and environment than about its impact on workers inside the plants.[11]

Over a period of decades, massive amounts of waste were released from the facilities at Oak Ridge into surrounding groundwater, streams, air, and shale formations beneath the plants. This waste disposal, hidden behind AEC and DOE secrecy, was not the cause of extensive debate until the 1980s. A combination of environmental and antinuclear activists brought the issue of environmental pollution of Oak Ridge into the open. In the introduction to his 1983 study *The Legacy of Oak Ridge: An Unclassified Briefing*, Albert Bates of the Natural Rights Center of Summertown, Tennessee, described Oak Ridge as "the territory in the United States of America where the feathers of sparrows set Geiger counters clicking at 26,000 counts per minute, where each gram of soil tested over several acres contains over 50 picocuries of plutonium, and where for the last forty years the creek and lake waters have exceeded state and Federal regulations for allowable radioactive pollution." His research indicated that the problems of radioactive pollution at Oak Ridge continued as a result of DOE's exemption from Federal and state environmental regulation. He noted that state radiation inspectors were not allowed by DOE to measure discharge into streams at the DOE's discharge pipes but instead took their measurements several miles away. Bates also argued that the scale of releases from Oak Ridge made it difficult to measure environmental pollution; there were more than one hundred different discharge pipes coming from the Y-12 plant alone. Much of the routine waste from Y-12 was, in 1983, still being pumped untreated into the environment after having been "diluted" in treatment ponds.[12]

At present, Oak Ridge ranks among the most polluted sites in the DOE system. According to Arjun Makhijani's worldwide study of atomic contamination, *Nuclear Wastelands*, there are more than six hundred contaminated sites at Oak Ridge that require remediation. Radiation and toxic chemicals—including uranium, plutonium, mercury, lead, chlorine, and petroleum—were released into the air, buried in the soil, discharged into surface water and pumped deep beneath the ground over the facilities' fifty-year life-span. More than 440,000 cubic meters of low-level nuclear waste were disposed of at Oak Ridge through 1991, and 41,000 cubic meters of mixed low-level waste were at the reservation in 1991.[13]

The sheer extent of environmental contamination at Oak Ridge makes the problem difficult to comprehend. The dumping of tons of untreated radioactive and chemically poisonous waste affected the entire community. For workers, this meant that living and working in Oak Ridge inflicted a double dose of radiation and hazardous chemicals—one in the plants and one from waste materials that escaped into the community. Even those who never set foot inside the plants were at risk from radiological and chemical hazards.

Closing the Books
THE DOE OWNS UP

In 1999, Secretary of Energy Bill Richardson admitted that the American nuclear weapons industry had harmed its workers through exposure to radiation and toxic chemicals. This announcement was hardly a surprise to workers or to those familiar with DOE safety practices. Yet Richardson's announcement was the first official confirmation of hazardous conditions that had long been denied by the agency. The question has become not whether workers were harmed by chemicals and radiation in the workplace, but the extent of the injury and how to best redress the damage.

"We are moving forward to do the right thing by these workers," Secretary Richardson said. "The men and women who served our nation in the nuclear weapons industries of World War II and the cold war labored under difficult and dangerous conditions with some of the most hazardous materials known to mankind. This is a fair and reasonable program. It will compensate workers and get them the help they have long deserved."[14]

The Department of Energy has confessed to its environmental problems as well. In the 1997 report *Linking Legacies*, the DOE admitted that it had discharged mercury into Oak Ridge waterways since 1950, totaling three-quarters of a million pounds. The area remains contaminated to this day, with higher than permitted amounts of mercury still present in the water. Mercury also was accidentally released into the soil around Oak Ridge plants, and mercury residues remain in pipes and sewers at Oak Ridge's Y-12 plant. Mercury vapors escaped the plant through the ventilation system, and spills at the plant were collected in basement sumps that emptied into storm sewers. Some of the mercury released to the environment is believed to be in the sludge at the bottom of the area's lakes and ponds.[15]

The DOE turned the issue of compensation for worker health problems over to the National Economic Council for review by a panel of experts drawn from several cabinet agencies. An interagency working group established to evaluate the workers' claims to compensation found "credible evidence of occupational illness in current and former workers at DOE facilities" and that DOE contract workers "have suffered material impairment of health as a result of performing their jobs." The study also pointed out that DOE's failure to record exposure of workers to chemical and other nonradiation hazards makes full knowledge of worker exposure and health impacts impossible.[16]

In 2000 and 2001, Congress passed two pieces of legislation to address atomic workers and head off lawsuits against the federal government and its contractors. PL 106-398: Energy Employees Occupational Illness Compensation Program Act of 2000 created a program to compensate workers $100,000 each for work-related injuries and diseases at atomic facilities, including Oak Ridge, plus medical care for all work-related health problems. Under the law, workers also would be eligible for state workers' compensation payments, if applicable. The payment was contingent on dropping all lawsuits against the federal government and contractors, and the measure served as an attempt to close the books on the health problems caused by the atomic weapons production process. Payment was raised to $150,000 in PL 107-107, Section 3151, Amendments to the Energy Employees Occupational Illness Compensation Program Act of 2000.

The past problems of the atomic production program continue to haunt efforts to remedy injuries to workers. For example, this program depends on DOE and contractor records of radiation exposure that simply may not exist. Of the 6,900 claims filed for the $150,000 payment in Tennessee with the Department of Labor, 1,609 were approved and 1,444 denied. The approval system is Byzantine, dependent on locating worker records, reconstructing possible exposure doses, reviewing medical histories to determine if an illness is likely to be caused by radiation, and consideration of other factors, such as smoking. The system also varies by site. Workers in K-25's gaseous diffusion plant were declared a special cohort in the legislation, with an assumption that their cancers were caused by radiation, while Y-12 and ORNL workers faced a more stringent standard. The program to provide workers' compensation has been even less effective at remuneration . The program has an almost astronomical rejection rate; of the 17,857 claims received nationally, 529 complete worker records were located and only 29 claims approved for payment.

Efforts to compensate Oak Ridge's workers have been a prisoner to the past. Oak Ridge's workers came from all over America, and many moved on during or after the war. Workers were never told of their exposure levels or even what they were being exposed to. Record keeping and safety took a backseat to production both during and after the war. All of these historical factors have worked against compensation of workers and their survivors.

Contested Patriotism

THE LANGUAGE OF PATRIOTISM that suffused Oak Ridge from its founding still resonates in the city. President Bill Clinton recognized this when he stated in an executive order:

> Since World War II, hundreds of thousands of men and women have served their Nation in building its nuclear defense. In the course of their work, they overcame previously unimagined scientific and technical challenges. Thousands of these courageous Americans, however, paid a high price for their service, developing disabling or fatal illnesses as a result of exposure to beryllium, ionizing radiation, and other hazards unique to nuclear weapons production and testing. Too often, these workers were neither adequately protected from, nor informed of, the occupational hazards to which they were exposed.[1]

Similar patriotic language was used by the daughter of a sick Oak Ridge worker at a DOE town meeting in 1999:

> I am the daughter of a man that worked after he came out of the service. They owned a grocery store out here in Oak Ridge called Kees grocery. And he was a patriotic person that served his country and he went to work for a place called AEC, Atomic Energy Commission, and X-10, which has just been touched on lightly. He was involved in a spill that they had out there and this is a photo of him that he was at work at and he was sent home immediately. And to show you how dangerous it was he was home for about six weeks, as I recall. . . . He was never taken back because he was told his radiation levels were too high. Big deal, you know, what did they do with him? Nothing. We lost our house, we lost everything that they had.[2]

Over the decades, patriotism has been used both as a means of keeping workers quiet and as a language to make demands on employers and the federal government. The contest over patriotism, and what it really means, continues at Oak Ridge to this day, as workers and their government continue to wrestle over what the nation owes Oak Ridge's workers for their sacrifice.

The story of Oak Ridge is not yet finished. Though the town faces economic and political hurdles to maintain its status as a science and technology-rich region, it is not in danger of complete shutdown, like the Paducah (Kentucky), Portsmouth (Ohio), and Hanford (Washington) sites. With a major national laboratory, a wide range of technologically advanced equipment, and a large, skilled workforce, Oak Ridge's future is not as bleak as that of many other areas of Tennessee, already abandoned by the coal, textile, and chemical industries. Even tourism is alive at Oak Ridge, as local museums and history tours have turned the area into a destination for those interested in atomic or World War II history.

The struggles of workers at these facilities for the promises that initially drew forbears to Oak Ridge—high wages, good working conditions, and a sense of community—will continue as well. While Congress and the executive branch both have pledged to pay back the workers who helped win World War II and the cold war, the programs thus far implemented have fallen short of these lofty goals. Unions in Oak Ridge have fought to maintain employment levels, even as the federal government and its contractors have sought to create a smaller, cheaper workforce.

Thousands of ordinary people came to Oak Ridge, constructed plants, built a community, helped make the atomic bomb, developed unions, established community groups, and created a city government. They grappled with issues of secrecy, patriotism, service, rights, and obligations to the government. They reshaped notions of patriotism, presented to them in propaganda posters, into a language to express their grievances and hopes for their community.

Founded to win World War II and kept in business by the cold war, Oak Ridge is, and continues to be, a laboratory for the meaning of patriotism in America. Its workers, residents, managers, and government officials wrestled with the issue of what it means to be patriotic, what demands are justified by service to the nation, how citizens' loyalty are abused by the government, and what rights must be given up to protect one's country. Long after the end of the cold war, these questions have gained new relevance as the United States grapples with terrorism at home and abroad.

Notes

Chapter 1

1. William Lawren, *The General and the Bomb* (New York: Dodd Mead, 1988).

2. For the battle over voting during and after World War II, see Cultice Wendell, *Youth's Battle for the Ballot* (Westport, Conn.: Greenwood Press, 1992).

3. For the general tone of World War II America, see John Morton Blum, *V Was for Victory: Politics and American Culture During World War II* (New York: Harcourt Brace Jovanovich, 1976). For the end of the New Deal, see Alan Brinkley, *The End of Reform: New Deal Liberalism in Recession and War* (New York: Knopf, 1995). For military development of the American South and West, see Ann Markusen et al., *The Rise of the Gunbelt: The Military Remapping of Industrial America* (New York: Oxford Univ. Press, 1991), and Bruce J. Schulman, *From Cotton Belt to Sunbelt: Federal Policy, Economic Development, and the Transformation of the South, 1938–1980* (New York: Oxford Univ. Press, 1991).

4. Theda Skocpol, *Protecting Soldiers and Mothers: The Political Origins of Social Policy in the United States* (Cambridge: Harvard Univ. Press, 1992). For use of military service as an argument for racial justice, see Ronald Takaki's *Double Victory: A Multicultural History of America in World War II* (Boston: Little, Brown, 2000).

5. "Transcript of Proceedings: 8 December 1999 Public Meeting with Dr. David Michaels, DOE Assistant Secretary of Energy for Environment, Safety and Health," 37–38, on line at DOE web site, http://www.eh.doe.gov/benefits.

6. Richard Hewlett and Oscar Anderson, *The New World: A History of the United States Atomic Energy Commission*, vol. 1, *1939–1946* (1962; reprint, Berkeley and Los Angeles: Univ. of California Press, 1990); Vincent Jones, *Manhattan: The Army and the Atomic Bomb* (Washington, D.C.: United States Army, 1985); Richard Hewlett and Francis Duncan, *Atomic Shield: A History of the United States Atomic Energy Commission*, vol. 2, *1947–52* (1962; reprint, Berkeley and Los Angeles: Univ. of California Press, 1990); Barton Hacker, *The Dragon's Tail* (Berkeley and Los Angeles: Univ. of California Press, 1987); Stephane Groueff, *Manhattan Project: The Untold Story of the Making of the Atomic Bomb* (Boston: Little, Brown, 1967); Robert Norris, *Racing for the Bomb: General Leslie S. Groves, the Manhattan Project's Indispensable Man* (South Royatton, Vt.: Steerforth Press, 2002); Barton Hacker, *Elements of Controversy: The Atomic Energy Commission and Radiation Safety in Nuclear Weapons Testing, 1947–74* (Berkeley and Los Angeles: Univ. of California

Press, 1994); George Mazuzan and J. Samuel Walker, *Controlling the Atom: The Beginnings of Nuclear Regulation, 1946–62* (Berkeley and Los Angeles: Univ. of California Press, 1985); J. Samuel Walker, *Containing the Atom: Nuclear Regulation in a Changing Environment* (Berkeley and Los Angeles: Univ. of California Press, 1992); J. Samuel Walker, *Permissible Dose: A History of Radiation Protection in the Twentieth Century* (Berkeley and Los Angeles: Univ. of California Press, 2000).

7. Thomas Hughes, *American Genesis: A Century of Invention and Technological Enthusiasm* (New York: Viking, 1989); Peter Bacon Hales, *Atomic Spaces: Living on the Manhattan Project* (Urbana: Univ. of Illinois Press, 1997); Charles Jackson and Charles Johnson, *City Behind a Fence: Oak Ridge, Tennessee, 1942–1946* (Knoxville: Univ. of Tennessee Press, 1981).

8. Those in search of more information on Oak Ridge's scientific and technological elite are advised to read Jackson and Johnson's *City Behind a Fence*, as that book draws on interviews of many of the leading scientists and engineers of the period. For scientific research at Oak Ridge, see Leland Johnson and Daniel Schaffer, *Oak Ridge National Laboratory: The First Fifty Years* (Knoxville: Univ. of Tennessee Press, 1994).

Chapter 2

Epigraph: Progress Report, Dept 186, Tennessee Eastman Corporation, 1945. Box 3, TEC Collection, RG 326, National Archives Regional Branch, East Point, Ga. (hereafter cited as TEC).

1. Charles Chamberlain, *Victory at Home: Manpower and Race in the American South, during World War II* (Athens: Univ. of Georgia Press, 2003), 96.

2. For a description of National War Labor Board practices, see National War Labor Board, *Termination Report* (Washington D.C.: Government Printing Office, 1947). For wage restrictions during World War II, see Jerome M. Staller and Loren M. Solnick, "Treatment of Escalators under Wage and Price Controls," in *Wage and Price Controls: The U.S. Experiment*, ed. John Kraft and Blaine Roberts (New York: Praeger, 1975), 70–79. See also Hugh Rockoff, *Drastic Measures: A History of Wage and Price Controls in the United States* (Cambridge: Cambridge Univ. Press, 1984).

3. Oak Ridge worker, interview with author, Oak Ridge, Tenn., Aug. 29, 1999.

4. Ibid.

5. Oak Ridge worker, interview with author, Oak Ridge, Tenn., Aug. 22, 1999.

6. United States Army, Manhattan Engineer District, "Manpower Needs," Entry 5, Box 46, Decimal File 201, RG 77, National Archives, College Park, Md.; United States War Manpower Commission, "Labor Market Development Report" (hereafter cited as LMDR), Dec. 15, 1943, p. 5, Box 11, Region 7, RG 211, National Archives Regional Branch, East Point, Ga. (hereafter cited as NA–East Point).

7. Leslie Groves, Diary, Groves Gift Collection, RG 200, National Archives, College Park, Md. (hereafter cited as GD); GD, June 19, 1944; GD, July 17, 1944.

8. LMDR, 8. From an interview conducted by Jackson and Johnson as part of their research for *City Behind a Fence*. They graciously allowed me to use the tapes in dissertation research. To protect the anonymity of the interview subjects, I have coded the interview data simply as Jackson and Johnson interview, followed by the date of the interview.

9. United States War Manpower Commission, "Advertising copy," Oct. 18, 1943, C530.2 Folder, Series 3, Box 10, Region 7, RG 211, NA–East Point.

10. Sullivan to Tate, June 14, 1943, Series 11, Box 3, Region 7, RG 211, NA–East Point; Ashe to White, July 6, 1943, Series 11, Box 3, Region 7, RG 211, NA– East Point.

11. Klugh to Ashe, Aug. 21, 1943, Series 11, Box 3, Region 7, RG 211, NA–East Point.

12. United States Army, Manhattan Engineer District, "Manning of Clinton Engineering Works," Jan. 12, 1944, Series 66A962, Box 14, Entry CEW 004.04, RG 326, NA–East Point.

13. T. E. Lane, "History of Union Carbide Corporation in the Atomic Energy Industry," unpublished ms., possession of Donald Lane, Oak Ridge, Tenn.

14. Tennessee Eastman Corporation, *CEW-TEC History, January 1943–May 1947* (Oak Ridge, Tenn., 1947), 27–28.

15. Medical Survey Group, Coal Mines Administration, United States Department of the Interior, *Medical Survey of the Bituminous Coal Industry,* Mar. 17, 1947 (Washington, D.C.: Government Printing Office, 1947).

16. Nichols to Chief of Engineers, Aug. 20, 1945, "Army E Award" Folder, Man 004.03, Entry 66A1405, Box 50, RG 326, NA–East Point.

17. Mel Fiske, "Atomic Workers," *CIO News Victory Edition,* June 24, 1946; Robeson to Shackelford, Sept. 21, 1943, Series 11, Box 3, Region 7, RG 211, NA–East Point.

18. Colleen Black, interview with Stanley Goldberg, video recording, Oak Ridge, Tenn., Mar. 3, 1987, Manhattan Project, Session 5, p. 59; videotape and transcript at Smithsonian Video History Program, Smithsonian Archive, Washington, D.C. (hereafter cited as Smithsonian Video History).

19. Tennessee Eastman Corporation, *CEW-TEC History,* 33 and 37; Carbide and Carbon Chemical Corporation, *First Annual Industrial Relations Report, Oak Ridge Plants, K-25, Y-12 and X-10, Fiscal Year 1949,* Atomic Energy Commission, RG 326, 67A1058, Box 138, National Archives and Records Administration, College Park, Md.

20. Oak Ridge worker, interview with author, Oak Ridge, Tenn., Aug. 22, 1999.

21. This paragraph draws on the research of Charles Jackson and Charles Johnson, whose *City Behind a Fence* remains the best source of information on the housing situation in Oak Ridge.

22. Black, Session 5, p. 59, Smithsonian Video History; Clarence Larson, Session 6, p. 19, Smithsonian Video History.

23. *Oak Ridge Journal,* Nov. 8, 1945.

24. Jackson and Johnson interview, Mar. 26, 1976; *Oak Ridge Journal,* Mar. 1, 1946.

25. Myers to McNutt, Aug. 20, 1943, Tennessee Folder, Series 10, Box 11, Region 7, RG 211, NA–East Point.

26. Andrew Kersten, *Race, Jobs and the War: The FEPC in the Midwest, 1941–1946* (Urbana: Univ. of Illinois Press, 2000).

27. Donald Lane, interview with author, Oak Ridge, Tenn.

28. Gail Radford, *Modern Housing for America: Policy Struggles in the New Deal Era* (Chicago: Univ. of Chicago Press, 1996); Arnold R. Hirsch, *Making the Second Ghetto: Race and Housing in Chicago, 1940–1960* (Cambridge: Cambridge Univ. Press, 1983).

29. Nancy Grant, *TVA and Black Americans* (Philadelphia: Temple Univ. Press, 1989), 53 and 55; K. Crandall Shifflett, *Coal Towns: Life, Work and Culture in Company Towns in Southern Appalachia, 1880–1960* (Knoxville: Univ. of Tennessee Press, 1991), 60–66; Jackson and Johnson interview, Apr. 3, 1976; Jackson and Johnson interview, May 1, 1976.

30. Robeson to Shackelford, Sept. 21, 1943, Series 11, Box 3, Region 7, RG 211, NA–East Point; Valeria Steele, "A New Hope" in *These Are Our Voices,* ed. J. Overhold (Knoxville: East Tennessee Historical Society, 1987), 200; Case 7-UR-75, Regional Files, Region 7–FEPC, Fair Employment Practices Committee, RG 228, NA–East Point; Closed Cases Collection, Box 4, International Union of Operating Engineers, Local 917 and 7-BR-177, J. A. Jones Company. In these cases, the FEPC investigated discrimination by AFL unions and the companies involved, which admitted to workplace segregation and discrimination. Both cases were closed without resolution by the FEPC.

31. Steele, "New Hope," 199; Garner to United States Employment Service, Oct. 18, 1943, C530.2 Folder, Series 3, Box 10, Region 7, RG 211, NA–East Point.

Chapter 3

1. Historian Nelson Lichtenstein describes these wartime strikes as the product of shop floor grievances that the labor bureaucracy ignored. At the forefront of these strikes was "the organic leadership" of factory workers; demands emerged from "rank and file militancy [that was] rooted in the concrete social and technical structures of the factory workplace." These striking workers did not view themselves as being against the war effort. Instead, many workers supported the no- strike pledge in principle but felt that when pushed too far, they had a right to strike in defense of their rights. This led to a "divided consciousness," or alternating sentiments of patriotism and grievance during the war.

Historian Joshua Freeman interprets these strikes differently, focusing on the vast majority of workers who continued laboring uninterrupted during the war. The real business of labor, according to Freeman, was "delivering the goods" to the soldiers at the front fighting the Nazis and Japanese. The people who did strike during World War II primarily were "green hands," new to industrial work, prone to actions "spontaneous, unchanneled, uncoordinated and untempered by larger union or political concerns." According to Freeman, these stoppages were motivated by individual greed or racism rather than worker solidarity.

The actions of construction and skilled trades workers at Oak Ridge do not fall cleanly into Freeman or Lichtenstein's historical interpretations. On the one hand, evidence of worker activism at Oak Ridge supports Lichtenstein's conclusions in several respects: Workers who walked off the job during World War II were the most experienced unionists, and their demands primarily treated working conditions and job control, not wages, hours, or racial composition of the labor force. However, Freeman is correct to conclude that, for the majority of workers, "delivering the goods" to the front was of the utmost importance, particularly to those with a long-term investment in their jobs. See Nelson Lichtenstein, "Auto Worker Militancy and the Structure of Factory Life, 1937–55," *Journal of American History* 67 (2): 335–53, 53. And Joshua Freeman, "Delivering the Goods: Industrial Unionism During World War II," *Labor History Reader* (Urbana: Univ. of Illinois Press, 1985), 401.

2. Lawren, *General and the Bomb*, and Jones, *Manhattan*, 354.

3. David F. Noble, "Command Performance: A Perspective on the Social and Economic Consequences of Military Enterprise," in *Military Enterprise and Technological Change*, ed. Merritt Roe Smith (Cambridge: MIT Press, 1985), 333. Groves's style is also well summarized in Norris, *Racing for the Bomb*.

4. John Ohly, "Formulation of Labor Policies to Govern Operation of C.E.W.," Nov. 10, 1944, Folder 80, Harrison-Bundy Papers, National Archives.

5. Ibid.

6. Ibid.

7. Ibid.

8. GD, Nov. 29, Dec. 12, 1944.

9. Jackson and Johnson interview, May 15, 1976.

10. William Cornelius to W. C. Brandan, July 28, 1944, Entry 66A962, Box 14, Decimal File CEW 004.04, "Industrial Mobilization," RG 326, NA–East Point (hereafter cited as "Industrial Mobilization"); Pope to Foremen, July 10, 1944, "Industrial Mobilization."

11. Sven Ekholm, July 14, 1944, "Industrial Mobilization."

12. Wikle to District Engineer, July 26, 1944; Williams to District Engineer, July 31, 1944; Whitaker to DE, July 25, 1944; Manning of CEW, Jan. 12, 1944, all in "Industrial Mobilization."

13. Wikle to District Engineer, n.d., enclosure; J. A. Jones to District Engineer, July 16, 1944, both in "Industrial Mobilization."

14. Appen to All Foremen, June 16, 1944; Appen to Superintendents, May 27, 1944; Appen to Truck Drivers, Apr. 7, 1944, all in "Industrial Mobilization."

15. Junkin to Wischmeyer, May 19, 1945, and "Review Board Report," May 21, 1945, "Crime" Folder, Decimal 000.5, RG 326, NA–East Point.

16. Jones, *Manhattan*, 376.

17. Strike data extracted from Jones, *Manhattan,* 371–76, and Labor Diary (hereafter cited as LD), 1943–45, passim.

18. LD, Aug. 1, 1945.

19. LD, Aug. 3, 1945.

20. C. T. Vettel, "Attempt to Organize Guard Personnel," Aug. 25, 1943, "ORBO-200.7" Folder, Declassified Files, 1943–60, Box 6, Oak Ridge Operations Office, Community Affairs Collection, RG 326, NA– East Point (hereafter cited as OROO-CA).

21. Statement of Leslie S. Carr, "080—IBEW" Folder, Box 74, RG 326, National Archives Regional Branch, Atlanta.

22. Ibid.

23. Jackson and Johnson interview, May 15, 1976.

24. Mattson to Kefauver, Aug. 22, 1949, Sept. 1949 Folder, Box 3, Entry 8, RG 326, National Archives, College Park, Md.

25. James M. Brown to L. C. Dolan, Feb. 9, 1945, "757 Gas Exposure," "Safety" Folder, Box 276, TEC.

Chapter 4

Epigraph: Olin Smith, "Comments," May 1946, "Smith v. Carbide and Carbon" Folder, Box 117, p. 6, Leo Goodman Papers, Manuscript Division, Library of Congress (hereafter cited as Goodman Papers).

1. Connie Bolling, Session 5, p. 42, Smithsonian Video History.

2. Black, Session 5, pp. 42 and 44, Smithsonian Video History; Larson, Session 6, p. 76, Smithsonian Video History.

3. Jackson and Johnson interview, July 24, 1976.

4. Black, Session 5, p. 44, Smithsonian Video History; "Audit," Entry 5, Box 52, Decimal File 319.1, MED, RG 77, National Archives, College Park, Md. This document is an audit of MP security division and lists the numbers and ranks of security and intelligence personnel throughout the project.

5. Jackson and Johnson interview, July 17, 1976; Jackson and Johnson interview, Mar. 25, 1976.

6. Jackson and Johnson interview, Apr. 3, 1976; Jackson and Johnson interview, July 24, 1976.

7. Parsons to Murphee, n.d., "Crime" Folder, RG 326.

8. Crime sample found in "Crime" Folder, RG 326.

9. Robert Livingston, Session 6, p. 68, Smithsonian Video History.

10. Black, Session 5, p. 32; Livingston, Session 6, p. 68; Chris Keim, Session 6, p. 88, all in Smithsonian Video History.

11. Bolling, Session 5, pp. 20 and 25; George Banic, Session 6, p. 69, Smithsonian Video History.

12. Black, Session 5, pp. 44–45 and 47, Smithsonian Video History.

13. Olin Smith, "Comments," May 1946, "Smith v. Carbide and Carbon" Folder, Box 117, p. 6, Goodman Papers.

14. Paul Vanstrum, Session 7, p. 24, Smithsonian Video History.

Chapter 5

1. U.S. Advisory Committee on Human Radiation Experiments, http://tis.eh.doe.gov/ohre/roadmap/achre/chap5_2.html.

2. Hacker, *Dragon's Tail*, 4, 57, 160. See also Mazuzan and Walker, *Controlling the Atom*, 37, and Hewlett and Anderson, *New World*. The documentary evidence contradicting the traditional interpretation of the Manhattan Project's safety record is drawn from public information releases in the Department of Energy's Oak Ridge Operation Office Public Reading Room, Oak Ridge, Tennessee. These documents have been declassified by DOE and placed in this collection for public access and review (hereafter cited as OROO-PRR and described by file type and series).

3. Charles Perrow, *Normal Accidents: Living with High-risk Technologies* (New York: Basic Books, 1984).

4. Diana Vaughan, *The Challenger Launch Decision: Risky Technology, Culture and Deviance at NASA* (Chicago: Univ. of Chicago, 1996), 66–67.

5. See Hacker, *Dragon's Tail*, 10–33; Claudia Clark, "Radium Poisoning Revealed: A Case Study in the History of Industrial Health Reform," *Humboldt Journal of Social Relations* 16, no. 2 (1991): 73–116; and Claudia Clark, *Radium Girls: Women and Industrial Health Reform, 1910–1935* (Chapel Hill: Univ. of North Carolina Press, 1997). These findings were documented in the papers of Harrison Martland, copies of which were used as the basis for Manhattan Project health and safety policy. See also Werner Schüttman, "Schneeberg Lung Disease and Uranium Mining in the Saxon Ore Mountains," *American Journal of Industrial Medicine* 23 (1993): 355–68, for a description of prewar knowledge of uranium mining's respiratory effects. Gilbert Whittemore, "The National Committee on Radiation Protection, 1928–1960" (Ph.D. diss., History of Science, Harvard Univ., 1986), 177; and Hacker, *Dragon's Tail*, 26–27.

6. Special Hazard Survey, 44-7-603, 1944, EH00182, OROO-PRR; Robert Stone to Members of Medical Division, Mar. 29, 1945, ES00199, OROO-PRR; Hacker, *Dragon's Tail*, 50.

7. Stone to Members of Medical Division.

8. Ibid.

9. Hacker, *Dragon's Tail*, 52; TEC Process Division Annual Report, 1945, A-1.700-1/DELREV, OROO-PRR.

10. Hacker, *Dragon's Tail*, 52; TEC Process Division Annual Report, 1945, A-1,700-1/DELREV, OROO-PRR; Robert Stone to Members of Medical Division, Mar. 29, 1945, ES00199, OROO-PRR.

11. "Minutes of Special Meeting of Central Safety Committee Held 12/11/43 to Discuss Activity Hazards," OROO-PRR.

12. "Oral History of Waldo E. Cohn," interviewed by Michael Yuffee and Thomas Fisher Jr., Oak Ridge, Tenn., Jan. 18, 1995, DOE-EH-4064, p. 17.

13. Ibid., 10, 18.

14. *Oral History of Karl Z. Morgan*, interviewed by Michael Yuffee and Marissa Caputo, Indian Springs, Fla., Jan. 7, 1995, DOE-EH-0475, pp. 5, 9.

15. Ibid., 10, 11.

16. Ibid., 17.

17. Ibid., 13.

18. M. D. Whitaker to E. J. Murphy, Sept. 2, 1994, 44-9-542 Production, ORF01762, OROO-PRR.

19. Coryell to Johnson, Jan. 13, 1945, ORFO1362, OROO-PRR; Waldo E. Cohn to W. C. Johnson, Jan. 13, 1945, ORFO0559, OROO-PRR. One slug refers to the fact that only one piece of plutonium should have been used at a time in 706-C, not ten.

20. John Wirth to M. D. Whitaker, Nov. 7, 1944, ORFO2535, OROO-PRR.

21. Simons to Morgan, July 26, 1945, ORFO2610, OROO-PRR; Testimony of Floyd Grizzell, ACHRE Panel Meeting, Knoxville, Tenn., Mar. 2, 1995, now found at http://www.gwu.edu/~nsarchiv.

22. Wirth to Whitaker, Nov. 7, 1944.

23. Y-12 was closed as an electromagnetic separation class only until 1947, when it was shut down. The plant was subsequently reopened under the management of Carbon and Carbide Chemicals Corporation but never again was used for electromagnetic separation.

24. Sterner to Warren, Dec. 22, 1943, and "Tentative Recommendations for Safe-Handling Procedures in the Y-12 Operation," both in "1943–4 ADM-Medical-Examinations, Lab Tests" Folder, Box 267, TEC.

25. W. W. Kelley to J. C. Hecker, Dec. 6, 1943, "Personnel Insurance" Folder, TEC.

26. J. C. Hecker to A. D. Calley, May 8, 1944, "Operations 1943–1944" Folder, Box 94, TEC.

27. A. G. Anderson, Henry Holtzclaw, and Elizabeth E. Scott, "Report on Safety and Housekeeping, February 25–March 10, 1945" and "February 11–24, 1945," "4.4 Safety Reports" Folder, Box 5, TEC.

28. John Coughlin, Pauline Roberts, and A. V. Hendrickson, "Report on Safety and Housekeeping, March 25–April 7," "4.4 Safety Reports" Folder, Box 5, TEC.

29. J. M. DallaValle to J. H. Sterner, "Report on T Concentrations, Buildings 9202, 9201-1 and 9204-1," July 5, 1945, "4.4 Safety Reports" Folder, Box 5, TEC.

30. G. W. Henderson to Milton Howle, "Safety Recommendations for Building 9202," "Chemical Safety" Folder, Box 185, TEC.

31. J. L. Patterson to W. W. Kelley, Sept. 18, 1944, "Chemical Safety" Folder, Box 185, TEC.

32. Milton O. Howle to J. H. Sterner, Feb. 16, 1944, "Accidents" Folder, Box 87, TEC.

33. "Monthly Progress Report, Department 185 Summary, July 28, 1944," "Ballard" Folder, Box 67, TEC.

34. G. W. Anderson memo, Nov. 9, 1944, "Personnel—Employment" Folder, Box 184, TEC; "Progress Report—Chemical Division—Dept 186, October 1944," Box 184, TEC.

35. J. M. DallaValle to J. H. Sterner, "Survey and Recommendations, Building 9206," Aug. 21, 1945, "4.4 Safety Reports" Folder, Box 5, TEC.

Chapter 6

1. Alice Kimball Smith, *A Peril and a Hope: The Scientists' Movement in America, 1945–47* (Chicago: Univ. of Chicago Press, 1965); Paul S. Boyer, *By the Bomb's Early Light: American Thought and Culture at the Dawn of the Atomic Age* (New York: Pantheon, 1985).

2. Oak Ridge worker, interview with author, Oak Ridge, Tenn., Aug. 22, 1999.

3. Connie Bolling, Session 5, p. 65, Smithsonian Video History.

4. Ibid., p. 69.

5. United States Army, Manhattan Engineer District, Robert Patterson, Address, Sept. 29, 1945, "Army E Award" Folder, Man 004.03, Entry 66A1405, Box 50, RG 326, NA–East Point.

6. United States Army, Manhattan Engineer District, Leslie Groves, Address, Sept. 29, 1945, "Army E Award" Folder, Man 004.03, Entry 66A1405, Box 50, RG 326, NA–East Point.

7. United States Army, Manhattan Engineer District, Nichols to McCord, Sept. 18, 1945, "Army E Award" Folder, Box 50, Entry 66A1405, RG 326, NA–East Point.

8. Jackson and Johnson interview, Apr. 3, 1976.

9. United States Army, Manhattan Engineer District, "Oak Ridge Census" Folder, Man 091.4, Box 74, RG 77, National Archives, College Park, Md.; Jackson and Johnson interview, May 15, 1976.

10. Jackson and Johnson interview, May 22, 1976; Jackson and Johnson interview, July 17, 1976; Clarence Larson, Session 6, p. 73, Smithsonian Video History.

11. Jackson and Johnson interview, Apr. 1976.

12. John Edwards to David Lilienthal, Oct. 20, 1947; "Community Management," Folder 10, Box 21, OROO-CA.

13. Franklin to Williams, Jan. 17, 1949, "Report on Progress of Investigation of Housing Irregularities," "Classified Documents (Misc)" Folder, Declassified Files, 1943–60, Box 7, OROO-CA.

14. James Terry to Mr. Kellar, Oct. 28, 1947, "Complaints," Box 1, Public Affairs Office, OROO-CA.

15. Lester Templeton to Estes Kefauver, Oct. 27, 1948, "Housing Complaints" Folder, OROO-CA.

16. Mary King to Housing, Mar. 15, 1948, "Housing—General," Folder 629/1, Box B054/28/4, OROO-CA.

17. Edwards and Sullivan to Dabney, Nov. 19, 1947, "Complaints" Folder, Box 1, Public Affairs Office, OROO-CA.

18. United States Army, Manhattan Engineer District, Finneran to Kirkpatrick, Jan. 7, 1946, Decimal File 330.14, RG 326, NA–East Point.

19. Kenneth Rush to E. Kefauver, Aug. 3, 1948, "Oak Ridge, Anderson County" Folder, Box 1, Kefauver Papers, University of Tennessee Special Collections, Knoxville.

20. *Chicago Defender*, Dec. 29, 1945.

21. Ibid.

22. *Chicago Defender*, Jan. 5, 1946. No black residents of Oak Ridge were quoted in Waters's article. However, Waters could not have researched and written his story without the help of the black community in Oak Ridge. It is probable that individual blacks did not want to attach their names to criticism of Oak Ridge out of fear of reprisal.

23. Roane-Anderson Company, Mar. 3, 1949, "Resume of Colored Housing Operations in Oak Ridge, Tennessee," "1948–1949" Folder, Box 21, Public Affairs Office, OROO-CA.

24. Report of the School Building Survey, Oak Ridge Schools, July 1952, Box 4, RG 326, Community Affairs Division, Program Analysis Section, Housing Reports, 43–56.

25. Jackson to Ford, Sept. 26, 1949, "Community Management-3" Folder, Box 20, OROO-CA.

26. Jackson and Johnson interview, Mar. 26, 1976

27. United States National Labor Relations Board, Joy to Flaherty, Sept. 6, 1945, "CEW-Unions" Folder, Man 080, Box 74, RG 326, NA–East Point.

28. United States Department of War, Patterson to Herzog, Mar. 22, 1946, "CEW-Unions" Folder, Man 080, Box 74, RG 326, NA–East Point.

29. United States Federal Mediation and Conciliation Service, C. C. Peek, "Progress Report (15 October 1945)" and "Final Report (20 November 1945)," Case 452-2869, Box 1712, FMCS Case Files, 1913–48, RG 280, National Archives, College Park, Md.

30. C. O. Brown et al. to Truman, Jan. 21, 1946, Case 452-2869, Box 1712, FMCS Case Files, 1913–48, RG 280, National Archives, College Park, Md.

31. United States, National Labor Relations Board, Case File 10-R-1717, Jan. 24, 1946, Entry 155, Box 4605, 1946, 10-R-1717, RG 25, National Archives, College Park, Md.

32. Baker to Dinwiddie, Feb. 28, 1945, Styles to Smith, Oct. 29, 1945, Case 10-R-1717, Box 4605, Entry 155, RG 25, National Archives, College Park, Md.

33. Styles to Smith, Oct. 29, 1945, Case 10-R-1665, Box 4605, Entry 155, RG 25, National Archives, College Park, Md.

34. McMillan to Styles, Nov. 13, 1945, Case 10-R-1665, Box 4605; Styles to McMillan, Nov. 15, 1945, Case 10-R-1665, Box 4605; Oliver to Styles, Dec. 13, 1945, Case 10-R-1665, Box 4605; Joy to Smith, Feb. 5, 1946, Case 10-C-1810, Box 4605, all in Entry 155, RG 25, National Archives, College Park, Md.

35. Jack Kelly, Progress Report, Feb. 12, 1946, Case 464-137, Box 1974, FMCS Case Files, 1913–48, RG 280, National Archives, College Park, Md.

36. United States, Federal Mediation and Conciliation Service, Kelly, "Final Report," Mar. 6, 1946, Case 464-137, Box 1974, FMCS Case Files, 1913–48, RG 280, National Archives, College Park, Md.

37. Styles and Kuthenau to Smith, Apr. 18, 1946, Case 10-C-1810, Box 4605, Entry 155, RG 25, National Archives, College Park, Md.

38. Patterson to Herzog, Mar. 22, 1946, "CEW-Unions" Folder, Man 080, Box 74, RG 326, NA– East Point.

Chapter 7

1. Thelma Present, *Dear Margaret: Letters from Oak Ridge to Margaret Mead* (Knoxville: East Tennessee Historical Society, 1985), 103.

2. Margaret R. Somers, "Citizenship and the Place of the Public Sphere: Law, Community and Political Culture in the Transition to Democracy," *American Sociological Review* 58 (Oct. 1993): 587–620. Robert Korstad and Nelson Lichtenstein describe the ways labor organization led to demand for greater citizenship rights in Detroit and Winston-Salem in their article "Opportunities Found and Lost: Labor, Radicals and the Early Civil Rights Movement," *Journal of American History* 75, no. 3 (Dec. 1988): 786–811.

3. Gary Gerstle, *Working-class Americanism: The Politics of Labor in a Textile City, 1914–1960* (New York: Cambridge Univ. Press, 1989,) 5, 8, 179, and 336; Lizabeth Cohen, *Making a New Deal: Industrial Workers in Chicago, 1919–1939* (New York: Cambridge Univ. Press, 1990), 254, 257, 289, 301 and 367.

4. Michael Goldfield, in *The Color of Politics*, argued that the strategy of the CIO right doomed Operation Dixie from the start. The four mistakes Goldfield cited are the failure to challenge local elites, lack of appeal to African American workers, the exclusion of left-wingers from the Operation Dixie staff, and the construction of a union bureaucracy rather than a union membership in the South. Robert Zieger contended in *The CIO, 1935–55* that Operation Dixie lacked the unions' financial support and enthusiasm. Timothy Minchin, in his *What Do We Need a Union For?* blamed the failure of southern union drives on the weakness and division of the Textile Workers' Union, the rising prosperity of non-unionized mill workers during World War II, and the failure of disastrous textile strikes in the early 1950s. In *Like Night and Day,* Daniel Clark found that the hostile postwar legal environment led to the destruction of two southern textile union locals that had grown and prospered since World War II. Barbara Griffith, in *The Crisis of the American Labor Movement,* argued that many northern organizers, when faced with initial resistance and lack of a major "galvanizing" victory, concluded that southern workers did not want unions and gave up. Taking a more race-centered approach, historian Michael Honey argued that the CIO failure to support the advancement of civil rights for African Americans in the South fatally hampered the organizing drive. Michael Goldfield, *The Color of Politics: Race and the Mainsprings of American Politics* (New York: New Press, 1997), 240–49; Robert Zieger, *The CIO: 1935–1955* (Chapel Hill: Univ. of North Carolina Press, 1995), 241; Timothy Minchin, *What Do We Need a Union For? The TWUA in the South, 1945–1955* (Chapel Hill: Univ. of North Carolina

Press, 1997); Daniel J. Clark, *Like Night and Day: Unionization in a Southern Mill Town* (Chapel Hill: Univ. of North Carolina Press, 1997); Barbara S. Griffith, *The Crisis of American Labor: Operation Dixie and the Defeat of the CIO* (Philadelphia: Temple Univ. Press, 1988), 170; Michael Honey, "Operation Dixie," *Labor History* 31, no. 3 (Spring 1990): 374, 378. For a sharp rejoinder to Honey, see Alan Draper, *Conflict of Interests: Organized Labor and the Civil Rights Movement in the South, 1954–1968* (Ithaca, N.Y.: ILR Press, 1994).

5. *The Atomic Worker*, July 24, 1946, Industrial Relations Collection, RG 326, NA– East Point (hereafter cited as *AW*); Tennessee Eastman Corporation, *CEW-TEC History*, 24.

6. *AW*, May 28, 1946; *AW*, June 26, 1946; James Barrett to William Green, June 14, 1946, Folder 14, Box 3, Barrett Collection, Southern Labor History Archives, Georgia State University, Atlanta (hereafter cited as Barrett Collection).

7. Present, *Dear Margaret*, 103.

8. Ophus A. Evans, "Letter to the editor," *Knoxville News-Sentinel*, May 30, 1946.

9. Atomic Workers Organizing Committee Press Release, May 24, 1946, Littauer Library Vertical Collection, Harvard University (hereafter cited as AWOC); United States Army, Manhattan Engineer District, Nelson to International Association of Machinists, May 23, 1946, "IAM" Folder, Box 74, RG 326, NA–East Point.

10. Fraser to Crawford, June 28, 1946, "CEW-Unions" Folder, Man 080, Box 74, RG 326, NA–East Point; see "CIO Meeting at Galesburg Hall," Oct. 11, 1946, "Labor Relations" Folder, Box 8, Declassified Files, 1943–60, OROO-CA.

11. Christopher to Huberman, May 15, 1946, Operation Dixie (hereafter cited as OD).

12. AWOC, Aug. 16, 1946.

13. "The Oak Ridge Workers Case," AWOC.

14. Ibid.

15. *AW*, July 10, 1946; *AW*, July 5, 1946.

16. *AW*, July 10, 1946.

17. *AW*, July 5, 1946; *AW*, July 10, 1946; *AW*, July 31, 1946.

18. *AW*, July 5, 1946.

19. "The Woman and Her Job at TEC," AWOC; "End TEC's Unhealthy Conditions," *AW*, Aug. 15, 1946.

20. See Case 7-UR-75, Regional Files, Region 7–FEPC, RG 228, NA–East Point. J. A. Jones and International Union of Operating Engineers, Local 917, Case 7-BR-177, Box 4, Closed Cases Collection, Regional Files, Region 7–FEPC, RG 228, NA–East Point. In both cases, the FEPC investigated discrimination by AFL unions and the companies involved, which admitted to workplace segregation and discrimination. Both cases were closed without resolution by the FEPC.

21. *AW*, July 17, 1946, and June 19, 1946.

22. "International Brotherhood of Electrical Workers," Folder 080, Box 14, RG 326, NA–East Point.

23. Barrett Radio Script, n.d., Folder 1, Box 4, Barrett Collection; *Knoxville Labor News* (hereafter cited as *KLN*), June 20, 1946.

24. *KLN,* Aug. 15, 1946; John Hand, speech, found in Folder 1, Box 4, Barrett Collection.

25. *KLN,* June 20, 1946; ATLC to Curtis Nelson, July 2, 1946, Folder 4, Box 3, Barrett Collection.

26. "Some Things Which the AFL Has Done for Workers of Oak Ridge," AFL press release, Industrial Relations Collection, RG 326, NA– East Point (hereafter cited as AFL). "You Be the Judge," AFL; "Women in Industry and the Home," AFL.

27. "A C&CCC Employee to Clark Center," Aug. 2, 1946, Folder 15, Box 3, Barrett Collection.

28. "Women in Industry and the Home; AFL Script, Folder 1, Box 4, Barrett Collection.

29. Barrett to Green, June 14, 1946, Folder 14, Box 3, Barrett Collection.

30. Barrett to Googe, Aug. 27, 1946, Folder 15, Box 3, Barrett Collection.

31. Barrett notes, n.d., Folder 1, Box 4, Barrett Collection.

32. "Management Notes," Folder 1, Box 4, Barrett Collection; Tennessee Eastman Corporation, "Charges Made by the Unions and Our Answers," Aug. 14, 1946, Folder 1, Box 4, Barrett Collection.

33. LD, Aug. 23, 1946.

34. Bittner to Christopher, Aug. 23, 1946, OD; *AW,* vol. 1, p. 15; AWOC, Sept. 5, 1946.

35. LD, Aug. 28, 1946; Tennessee Eastman Corporation, *CEW-TEC History,* 64.

36. LD, Sept. 13, 1946.

37. U.S. Congress, Joint Committee on Atomic Energy, *Labor Policy in Atomic Energy Plants* (Washington, D.C.: Government Printing Office, 1948), 127.

Chapter 8

1. For the labor history of the wartime and postwar eras, useful accounts include George Lipsitz, *Rainbow at Midnight: Labor and Culture in the 1940s* (Urbana : Univ. of Illinois Press, 1994); John Howell Harris, *The Right to Manage: Industrial Relations Policies of American Business in the 1940s* (Madison: Univ. of Wisconsin Press, 1982); Nelson Lichtenstein, *Labor's War at Home: The CIO in World War II* (Cambridge: Cambridge Univ. Press, 1982); Nelson Lichtenstein, *The Most Dangerous Man in Detroit: Walter Reuther and the Fate of American Labor* (New York: Basic Books, 1995); and R. Alton Lee, *Truman and Taft-Hartley: A Question of Mandate* (Lexington: Univ. of Kentucky Press, 1966).

2. This impasse in collective bargaining does not support the argument of legal historian Christopher Tomlins that New Deal and postwar federal intervention in labor relations has been unfavorable to workers, bestowing a

"counterfeit liberty" on unions and workers. Instead, as Melvyn Dubofsky and Robert Zieger have argued, postwar political and legal developments restricted the power of unions, as federal power restrained rather than supported workers in their organizing and bargaining struggles. This shift from New Deal to postwar labor policy can be seen in the careers of several key figures in the federal government. Christopher Tomlins, *The State and the Unions: Labor Relations, Law and the Organized Labor Movement in America, 1880–1960* (Cambridge: Cambridge Univ. Press, 1985); Melvyn Dubofsky, *The State and Labor in Modern America* (Chapel Hill: Univ. of North Carolina Press, 1995); Zieger, *CIO.*

3. *CIO News*, Apr. 7, 1946, 12.

4. David Lilienthal, *Journals of David Lilienthal*, vol. 1, *The TVA Years* (New York: Harper and Row, 1964), 9.

5. Lilienthal, *Journals,* 597.

6. David Lilienthal, "Points to be Made in Discussion with AFL Group on X-10 Situation Tuesday," May 4, 1948, "Oak Ridge Labor Dispute" Folder, Box 11, Entry E1, RG 326, National Archives, College Park, Md.

7. United States Atomic Energy Commission, "History of Labor Relations," 9, "Carbide and Carbon" Folder, Box 4, Entry 87-07, RG 326, NA–East Point.

8. United States Atomic Energy Commission, "History of Labor Relations," 13, 14, 17. Monsanto explained that this high rate was needed to "compensate for the hazard factor." This "hazard factor" is suggestive of the way in which AFL unions viewed health issues (workers should be paid more for hazardous work), but the contract said nothing about means of reducing these hazards. Ibid., 7, 18.

9. Garrison, Morse, and Taylor to AEC, Jan. 4, 1947, 13, "AEC Labor" Folder, Box 35, RG 126, National Archives, College Park, Md.

10. Lackey to Swisher, Mar. 25, 1955, Folder 14, Box 205, Goodman Papers.

11. University of California Folder, Industrial Personnel Files, Box 1, RG 326, NA–East Point.

12. Eloise Stewart, "Bargaining History," July 20, 1946, 46, Case 474-965, Box 2209, RG 280, National Archives, College Park, Md.; LD, Aug. 19 and 21, 1947.

13. LD, Sept. 1–2, 1947.

14. Ibid.

15. "Will Carbide Accept Arbitration," Sept. 11, 1947, Case 474-965, Box 2209, FMCS Case Files, 1913–48, RG 280, National Archives, College Park, Md. Reports of Earle's autopsy appeared in newspapers, and the AEC examined Earle's corpse and declared him free of radiation, blaming the autopsy's radiation count on fluctuations of background radiation (*Oak Ridge Journal,* Aug. 21, 1947). The AEC stated that while the cause of Earle's death was unknown, it was not linked to radiation. This case, the first national report of a worker's death linked to radiation was a red flag to unionists at Oak Ridge, but the AEC was able to contain the damage with their in-house investigation and reports.

16. "Strike Vote Perils U.S. Atomic Output," *New York Times,* Dec. 6, 1947, p. 9; "Union Head Approves CIO Atom-Strike Vote," *New York Times,* Dec. 7, 1947, p. 38.

17. John Greene and Glen Neely to David Lilienthal, Jan. 7. 1948, "Correspondence—Labor" Folder, Box 8, Entry E1, RG 326, National Archives, College Park, Md.

18. U.S. Board of Inquiry Created by E.O. 9334, "Report to the President on the Labor Dispute at Oak Ridge National Laboratory, March 15, 1948," pp. 12 , 14, Folder 407B, Box 1189, Harry S. Truman Office Files, Harry S. Truman Library and Archives, Independence, Mo.

19. Ibid.

20. IPD Files, Box 1, University of California Folder, RG 326; Labor Relations, Nov. 18, 1947; U.S. Board of Inquiry, 23. NA–East Point.

21. Victor Reisel, "Inside Labor," *New York Post,* Mar. 9, 1948.

22. Ibid.

23. Ibid.

24. "Temporary Injunction of Justice George O. Taylor," "004.07 Carbide and Carbon Chemical Corporation—Labor" Folder, Box 14, Entry 67A803, RG 326, NA–East Point.

25. Weber to Joint Committee on Atomic Energy, Mar. 10, 1948, "Oak Ridge Labor" Folder, Box 492, RG 126, National Archives, College Park, Md.

26. AFL to Lilienthal, "Oak Ridge Labor Dispute" Folder, Box 11, Entry E1, RG 326, National Archives, College Park, Md.

27. "Changes in Rates of Hourly Workers since the Start of Collective Bargaining, Dec 1946–1953," Declassified Files, 1943–60, Box 2, OROO-CA.

28. For details of the rent movement in Oak Ridge, see "Oak Ridge—Housing and Rent" Folders 1 and 2, Box 87, Goodman Papers.

29. For details of the rent movement in Oak Ridge, see "Oak Ridge—Housing and Rent" Folders 1 and 2, Box 87, Goodman Papers.

30. For details of the rent movement in Oak Ridge, see ibid.

31. Details on union involvement in civil rights issues in Oak Ridge can be found in "Oak Ridge—Job Discrimination" Folder, Box 90, Goodman Papers.

32. For problems in Clinton, see Janice M. McClelland, "A Structural Analysis of Desegregation: Clinton High School, 1954–1958," *Tennessee Historical Quarterly* 56, no. 4 (Winter 1997): 296–309.

33. Elizabeth Peele, *A History of Segregation in Oak Ridge, 1943–1960* (Oak Ridge, Tenn.: Oak Ridge Community Relations Council, 1960).

Chapter 9

Epigraph: "Transcript of Proceedings: 8 December 1999 Public Meeting with Dr. David Michaels, DOE Assistant Secretary of Energy for Environment, Safety and Health," 31.

1. Olin Smith, "Comments," May 1946, "Smith v. Carbide and Carbon" Folder, Box 117, Goodman Papers.

2. Ibid.

3. Transcript: Olin G. Smith v. Carbide and Carbon Chemicals Corporation, Civil No. 848, "Smith v. Carbide and Carbon" Folder, Box 117, Goodman Papers.

4. "Insurance, 1946," ORAU 1433, OROO-PRR.

5. Ibid.

6. Oak Ridge worker, interview with author, Oak Ridge, Tenn., Aug. 20, 1999.

7. For examples, see Christopher Sellers, *Hazards on the Job: From Industrial Disease to Environmental Health Science* (Chapel Hill: Univ. of North Carolina Press, 1997); David Rosner and Gerald Markowitz, *Deadly Dust: Silicosis and the Politics of Occupational Disease in Twentieth-Century America* (Princeton, N.J.: Princeton Univ. Press, 1991); David Rosner and Gerald Markowitz, eds., *Dying for Work: Workers' Safety and Health in Twentieth Century America* (Bloomington: Indiana Univ. Press, 1987); and Helen Sheehan and Richard Wedeen, eds., *Toxic Circles: Environmental Hazards from the Workplace to the Community* (New Brunswick, N.J.: Rutgers Univ. Press, 1993).

8. United States Army, Manhattan Engineer District, Robinson to Groves, Mar. 15, 1945, Folder 700.2, "Medical Research of Bomb Casualties," Entry 5, Box 182, RG 77, National Archives, College Park, Md.

9. Ibid.; United States Atomic Energy Commission, Brundage to Marshall, May 15, 1947, ORFO0245, OROO-PRR; United States Atomic Energy Commission, Brundage to Marshall, May 15, 1947, ORFO0245, OROO-PRR.

10. United States Atomic Energy Commission, Batson to Young, Mar. 21, 1947, ORAU 1531, OROO-PRR.

11. Ibid., 31-32.

12. Ibid., 128-29.

13. Ibid., 129-30.

14. Ibid., 108-9.

15. James Brown to L. Z. Dolan, Feb. 9, 1945, "Safety" Folder, Box 276, TEC.

16. Personnel by Divisions, Aug. 25, 1945, "Personnel" Folder, Box 274, TEC.

17. TEC Injury Reports, Dec. 13, 1946. Since names were blacked out of these documents upon declassification, I have simply referred to them by accident date. TEC Injury Reports, Nov. 4, 1946.

18. TEC Injury Reports, May 2, 1946, Nov. 20, 1946, Apr. 15, 1946, and Dec. 31, 1945.

19. TEC Injury Reports, Oct. 12 , 1945, Sept. 27, 1945, Aug. 29, 1945, June 5, 1946, and Feb. 15, 1947.

20. James Brown to F. R. Conklin, Sept. 12, 1945, "Safety" Folder, Box 15, TEC.

21. Close to Taney, July 25, 1945, ORO 1178, 1, OROO-PRR.

22. Lilienthal to Celler, Apr. 14, 1949, "April 1949" Folder, Box 1, Entry 9, RG 326. See also Lilienthal to Celler, July 14, 1949, "July" Folder, Box 2, Entry 9, RG 326. NARA–College Park.

23. TEC Injury Reports, Nov. 20, 1945.

24. AEC Safety and Health Advisory Board, *Report,* Apr. 2, 1948, 16, ORFO-0544-PRR.

Chapter 10

1. Hermann Muller, "Time Bombing Our Descendants," *American Weekly,* Nov. 1946, 178, Muller Manuscripts, Hermann Muller Papers, Lilly Library, Indiana University, Bloomington (hereafter cited as Muller Papers).

2. Hermann Muller, "Some Present Problems in the Genetic Effects of Radiation," 196, Muller Papers.

3. For examples of classification of radiation data, see Robinson to Groves, Mar. 15, 1945, Folder 700.2, "Medical Research of Bomb Casualties," Box 182, Entry 5, RG 77, National Archives, College Park, Md.; Batson to Young, Mar. 21, 1947, ORAU 1531, OROO-PRR; Brundage to Marshall, May 15, 1947, ORFO0245, OROO-PRR; Jack Moshman, "On the Incidence of Cancer in Oak Ridge, Tennessee," July 2, 1948, Abstract, ORAU 1046, OROO-PRR. Moshman admitted that his study was preliminary in nature and limited by the scarcity of solid data, noting, "The people of Oak Ridge present a very mobile and atypical group. . . . Suffice it to say that inasmuch as people were continually moving off the area . . . it was manifestly next to impossible to trace all of the emigrant population for subsequent cancer deaths." Personnel data was also hard to come by, and Moshman admitted that "there is no accurate data pertaining to the turnover of personnel." Instead, he estimated the population of Oak Ridge from the number of employee badges rather than a detailed census.

4. For a history of the fallout debate, see Robert A. Divine, *Blowing on the Wind: The Nuclear Test Ban Debate, 1954–1960* (New York: Oxford Univ. Press, 1978).

5. Ernest Sternglass, *Secret Fallout* (New York: McGraw-Hill, 1981), 42.

6. Thomas Mancuso, Alice Stewart, and George Kneal, "Radiation Exposure of Hanford Workers Dying from Cancer and Other Causes," *Health Physics* 33 (Nov. 1977): 369–85; John W. Gofman, "The Question of Radiation Causation of Cancer in Hanford Workers," *Health Physics* 37 (Nov. 1979): 638. Mancuso's terminated AEC contract provoked a storm of criticism in the 1970s, but his work was ended by the AEC before his report was issued, due to issues of time and budget overruns of the entire effort.

7. Ethel Gilbert et al., "Mortality of Workers at the Hanford Site," *Health Physics* 56 (Jan. 1989): 11–25; John Acquavella et al., "Mortality Among Workers at the Pantex Weapons Facility," *Health Physics* 48 (June 1985): 735–46.

8. Physicians for Social Responsibility, *Dead Reckoning: A Critical Review of the Department of Energy's Epidemiological Research* (Washington, D.C.: Physicians for Social Responsibility), 61–62.

9. Harvey Checkoway, in a 1985 study of Oak Ridge National Laboratory (formerly X-10), linked workplace exposure to chemicals and radiation to

cancer. He found that those workers in engineering and maintenance had higher levels of cancer than expected. The study also found non-statistically significant but elevated levels of Hodgkin's disease, leukemia, and cancer of the prostate. In a 1988 study of the Y-12 plant, Checkoway found "mortality excess from of lung and brain and central nervous system cancers." University of North Carolina epidemiologist Steven Wing, in a far more detailed analysis than the AEC or DOE had ever conducted, examined death rates at Oak Ridge National Laboratory comparing the mortality of white-collar and blue-collar employees. Wing found that leukemia deaths were higher than would be expected for Oak Ridge workers, and that cancer deaths were statistically related to the exposure of workers to radiation. See Harvey Checkoway et al., "Radiation, Work Experience, and Cause Specific Mortality among Workers at an Energy Research Laboratory," *British Journal of Industrial Medicine* 42 (Aug. 1985): 525–33; Harvey Checkoway et al., "Radiation Dose and Cause-Specific Mortality among Workers at a Nuclear Materials Fabrication Plant," *American Journal of Epidemiology* 127 (Feb. 1988): 255–66; Steven Wing et al., "Mortality among Workers at ORNL," *Journal of the American Medical Association* 265 (Mar. 20, 1991): 1397–1402; and Steven Wing et al., "Job Factors, Radiation and Cancer Mortality at ORNL: Follow up through 1984," *American Journal of Industrial Medicine* 23 (Feb. 1993): 265–79.

10. Joseph Mangano, "Cancer Mortality Near Oak Ridge, Tennessee," *International Journal of Health Services* 24 (1994): 521 and 532. DOE researcher Charles McRae Sharpe contested Mangano's claim that cancer death rates have substantially increased in Oak Ridge. Charles McRae Sharpe, "Comments on 'Cancer Mortality Near Oak Ridge, Tennessee,'" *International Journal of Health Services* 25 (1995): 333–34. See Mangano's reply: Mangano, "A Response to Sharpe's Comments," *International Journal of Health Services,* 25 (1995): 345–49. Data from Anderson County show that cancer deaths have been on the upswing since the early 1980s, though the degree of difference, if any, between "actual" and statistically "expected" cancer deaths is still a matter of debate.

11. Barry Commoner, *The Closing Circle: Nature, Man, and Technology* (New York: Knopf, 1971).

12. Albert Bates, *The Legacy of Oak Ridge: An Unclassified Briefing* (Summertown, Tenn.: Natural Rights Canter, 1983), 1, 15, and 16.

13. Arjun Makhijani, Howard Hu, and Katherine Yih, *Nuclear Wastelands: A Global Guide to Nuclear Weapons Production and Its Health and Environmental Effects* (Cambridge, Mass.: MIT Press, 1995).

14. On line at http://tis.eh.doe.gov/portal/feature/pr00103.htm.

15. U.S. Department of Energy, *Linking Legacies: Connecting the Cold War Nuclear Weapons Production Process to Their Environmental Consequences* (Washington, D.C.: Government Printing Office, 1997), 136–47.

16. National Economic Council, Interagency Working Group, "The Link Between Exposure to Occupational Hazards and Illnesses in the Department of Energy Contract Workforce," 1–2, http://www.eh.doe.gov/benefits.

Conclusion

1. Executive Order 13179: Providing Compensation to America's Nuclear Weapons Workers.

2. "Transcript of Proceedings: 8 December 1999 Public Meeting with Dr. David Michaels, DOE Assistant Secretary of Energy for Environment, Safety and Health," 112–13.

Bibliography

Balogh, Brian. Chain Reaction: Expert Debate and Political Participation in American Civilian Nuclear Power, 1945–75. Cambridge: Cambridge Univ. Press, 1991.

Bates, Albert. The Legacy of Oak Ridge, An Unclassified Briefing. Summertown, Tenn.: Natural Rights Center, 1983.

Blum, John Morton. V Was for Victory: Politics and American Culture During World War II. New York: Harcourt Brace Jovanovich, 1976.

Boris, Eileen, and Nelson Lichtenstein. Major Problems in the History of American Workers. Lexington, Mass.: D. C. Heath,1991.

Boyer, Paul. By the Bomb's Early Light: American Thought and Culture at the Dawn of the Atomic Age. New York: Pantheon Books, 1985.

Braverman, Harry. Labor and Monopoly Capital: The Degradation of Work in the Twentieth Century. New York: Monthly Review Press, 1974.

Brinkley, Alan. The End of Reform: New Deal Liberalism in Recession and War. New York: Knopf, 1995.

Brody, David. Workers in Industrial America: Essays on the Twentieth Century Struggle. New York: Oxford Univ. Press, 1980.

Burawoy, Michael. Manufacturing Consent: Changes in the Labor Process Under Monopoly Capitalism. Chicago: Univ. of Chicago Press, 1979.

Burchett, Wilfred. Shadows of Hiroshima. London: Verso, 1983.

Caufield, Catherine. Multiple Exposures: Chronicles of a Radiation Age. New York: Harper and Row, 1989.

Chamberlain, Charles. Victory at Home: Manpower and Race in the American South, during World War II. Athens: Univ. of Georgia Press, 2003.

Clark, Claudia. Radium Girls: Women and Industrial Health Reform, 1910–1935. Chapel Hill: Univ. of North Carolina Press, 1997.

Clark, Daniel J. Like Night and Day: Unionization in a Southern Mill Town. Chapel Hill: Univ. of North Carolina Press, 1997.

Cohen, Lizabeth. Making a New Deal: Industrial Workers in Chicago, 1919–1939. Cambridge: Cambridge Univ. Press, 1990.

Committee for the Compilation of Materials on Damage Caused by the Atomic Bombs at Hiroshima and Nagasaki. Hiroshima and Nagasaki: The Physical, Medical, and Social Effects of the Atomic Bombings. New York: Basic Books, 1981.

Commoner, Barry. The Closing Circle: Nature, Man, and Technology. New York: Knopf, 1971.

Divine, Robert A. Blowing on the Wind: The Nuclear Test Ban Debate, 1954–1960. New York: Oxford Univ. Press, 1978.

Draper, Alan. Conflict of Interests: Organized Labor and the Civil Rights Movement in the South, 1954–1968.

Dubofsky, Melvyn. The State and Labor in Modern America. Chapel Hill: Univ. of North Carolina Press, 1991.

Fairchild, Byron, and Jonathan Grossman. The Army and Industrial Manpower. Washington, D.C.: Office of the Chief of Military History, Dept. of the Army, 1959.

Fine, Lenore, and Jesse Remington. The Corp of Engineers: Construction in the United States. Washington, D.C.: United States Army, 1972.

Gerstle, Gary. Working-Class Americanism: The Politics of Labor in a Textile City, 1914–1960. New York: Cambridge Univ. Press, 1989.

Gersuny, Carl. Work Hazards and Industrial Conflict. Hanover, N.H.: Univ. Press of New England, 1981.

Glaberman, Martin. Wartime Strikes: The Struggle Against the No-Strike Pledge in the UAW During World War II. Detroit: Bedwick Editions, 1980.

Goldfield, Michael. The Color of Politics: Race and the Mainsprings of American Politics. New York: New Press, 1997.

Graebner, William. Coal Mining Safety in the Progressive Period. Lexington: Univ. Press of Kentucky, 1976.

Grant, Nancy. TVA and Black Americans. Philadelphia: Temple Univ. Press, 1989.

Griffith, Barbara. The Crisis of American Labor: Operation Dixie and the Defeat of the C.I.O. Philadelphia: Temple Univ. Press, 1988.

Groueff, Stephane. Manhattan Project: The Untold Story of the Making of the Atomic Bomb. Boston: Little, Brown, 1967.

Groves, Leslie. Now It Can Be Told. New York: Harper and Row, 1962.

Hacker, Barton. The Dragon's Tail: Radiation Safety and the Manhattan Project, 1942–46. Berkeley: Univ. of California Press, 1987.

———. Elements of Controversy: The Atomic Energy Commission and Radiation Safety in Nuclear Weapons Testing, 1947–74. Berkeley and Los Angeles: Univ. of California Press, 1994.

Hales, Peter Bacon. Atomic Spaces: Living on the Manhattan Project. Urbana: Univ. of Illinois Press, 1997.

Harris, John Howell. The Right to Manage: Industrial Relations Policies of American Business in the 1940s. Madison: Univ. of Wisconsin Press, 1982.

Hewlett, Richard G., and Oscar Anderson. The New World: A History of the United States Atomic Energy Commission, 1939–1946. 1962. Reprint, Berkeley and Los Angeles: Univ. of California Press 1990.

Hewlett, Richard, and Francis Duncan. Atomic Shield: A History of the Atomic Energy Commission, 1946–1952. 1962. Reprint, Berkeley and Los Angeles: Univ. of California Press, 1990.

Hirsch, Arnold R. Making the Second Ghetto: Race and Housing in Chicago, 1940–1960. Cambridge: Cambridge Univ. Press, 1983.

Hoddeson, Lillian, Paul Henrikson, Roger Meade, and Catherine Westfall. Critical Assembly: A Technical History of Los Alamos During the Oppenheimer Years, 1943–1945. Cambridge: Cambridge Univ. Press, 1993.

Honey, Michael. Southern Labor and Black Civil Rights: Organizing Memphis Workers. Urbana: Univ. of Illinois Press, 1993.

Hughes, Thomas. American Genesis: A Century of Invention and Technological Enthusiasm. New York: Viking, 1989.

Johnson, Charles, and Charles Jackson. City Behind a Fence. Knoxville: Univ. of Tennessee Press, 1981.

Johnson, Leland, and Daniel Schaffer. Oak Ridge National Laboratory: The First Fifty Years. Knoxville: Univ. of Tennessee Press, 1994.

Jones, Vincent. Manhattan: The Army and the Atomic Bomb. Washington, D.C.: United States Army, 1985.

Kersten, Andrew. Race, Jobs and the War: The FEPC in the Midwest, 1941–1946. Urbana: Univ. of Illinois Press, 2000.

Kohn, Howard. Who Killed Karen Silkwood? New York: Summit Books, 1981.

Kraft, John, and Blaine Roberts, eds. Wage and Price Controls: The U.S. Experiment. New York: Praeger, 1975.

Lang, Daniel. Early Tales of the Atomic Age. New York: Doubleday, 1948.

Lawren, William. The General and the Bomb. New York: Dodd Mead, 1988.

Lee, R. Alton. Truman and Taft-Hartley: A Question of Mandate. Lexington: Univ. of Kentucky Press, 1966.

Lichtenstein, Nelson. Labor's War at Home: The CIO in World War II. Cambridge: Cambridge Univ. Press, 1982.

———. The Most Dangerous Man in Detroit: Walter Reuther and the Fate of American Labor. New York: Basic Books, 1995.

Lilienthal, David. The Journals of David Lilienthal. New York: Harper and Row, 1964.

Lipsitz, George. Rainbow at Midnight: Labor and Culture in the 1940s. Urbana: Univ. of Illinois Press, 1994.

Makhijani, Arjun, Howard Hu, and Katherine Yih. Nuclear Wastelands: A Global Guide to Nuclear Weapons Production and Its Health and Environmental Effects. Cambridge, Mass.: MIT Press, 1995.

Markusen, Ann, Peter Hall, Scott Campbell, and Deitrick Sabrina. The Rise of the Gunbelt: The Military Remapping of Industrial America. New York: Oxford Univ. Press, 1991.

Mazuzan, George, and J. Samuel Walker. Controlling the Atom: The Beginnings of Nuclear Regulation, 1946–62. Berkeley and Los Angeles: Univ. of California Press, 1985.

Medical Survey Group, Coal Mines Administration, United States Department of the Interior, Medical Survey of the Bituminous Coal Industry. Mar. 17, 1947. Washington, D.C.: Government Printing Office, 1947.

Minchin, Timothy. What Do We Need a Union For? The TWUA in the South, 1945–1955. Chapel Hill: Univ. of North Carolina Press, 1997.

National War Labor Board. Termination Report. Washington D.C.: Government Printing Office, 1947.

Nelkin, Dorothy, and Michael Brown. Workers at Risk: Voices from the Workplace. Chicago: Univ. of Chicago Press, 1984.

Noble, David. America by Design: Science, Technology and the Rise of Corporate Capitalism. New York: Knopf, 1987.

————. Forces of Production: A Social History of Industrial Automation. New York: Oxford Univ. Press, 1986.

Orlans, Harold. Contracting for Atoms. Washington, D.C.: Brookings Institution, 1967.

Peele, Elizabeth. A History of Segregation in Oak Ridge, 1943–1960. Oak Ridge, Tenn.: Oak Ridge Community Relations Council, 1960.

Perrow, Charles. Normal Accidents: Living with High-risk Technologies. New York: Basic Books, 1984.

Physicians for Social Responsibility. Dead Reckoning: A Critical Review of the Department of Energy's Epidemiological Research. Washington, D.C.: Physicians for Social Responsibility, 1992.

Present, Thelma. Dear Margaret: Letters from Oak Ridge to Margaret Mead. Knoxville: East Tennessee Historical Society, 1985.

Radford, Gail. Modern Housing for America: Policy Struggles in the New Deal Era. Chicago: Univ. of Chicago Press, 1996.

Rockoff, Hugh. Drastic Measures: A History of Wage and Price Controls in the United States. Cambridge: Cambridge Univ. Press, 1984.

Rosner, David, and Gerald Markowitz. Deadly Dust: Silicosis and the Politics of Occupational Disease in Twentieth Century America. Princeton, N.J.: Princeton Univ. Press, 1991.

————, eds. Dying for Work: Workers' Safety and Health in Twentieth Century America. Bloomington: Indiana Univ. Press, 1987.

Rosswurm, Steven, ed. The CIO's Left-Led Unions. New Brunswick, N.J.: Rutgers Univ. Press, 1992.

Sanger, S. L., and Robert Mull. Hanford and the Bomb: An Oral History of World War II. Seattle: Living History Press, 1989.

Schrecker, Ellen. The Age of McCarthyism: A Brief History with Documents. New York: Bedford Books, 1994.

Schulman, Bruce J. From Cotton Belt to Sunbelt: Federal Policy, Economic Development, and the Transformation of the South, 1938–1980. New York: Oxford Univ. Press, 1991.

Seaborg, Glenn. The Plutonium Story: The Journals of Professor Glenn T. Seaborg, 1939–1949. Columbus: Battelle Memorial Institute, 1994.

Sellers, Christopher. Hazards on the Job: From Industrial Disease to Environmental Health Science. Chapel Hill: Univ. of North Carolina Press, 1997.

Serwer, Daniel. "The Rise of Radiation Protection: Science, Medicine and Technology in Society, 1896–1935." Ph.D. diss., History of Science, Princeton Univ., 1977.

Sheehan, Helen, and Richard Wedeen, eds. Toxic Circles: Environmental Hazards from the Workplace to the Community. New Brunswick, N.J.: Rutgers Univ. Press, 1993.

Sherwin, Martin. A World Destroyed. New York: Vintage, 1987.

Shifflett, K. Crandall. Coal Towns: Life, Work and Culture in Company Towns in Southern Appalachia, 1880–1960. Knoxville: Univ. of Tennessee Press, 1991.

Skocpol Theda. Protecting Soldiers and Mothers: The Political Origins of Social Policy in the United States. Cambridge: Harvard Univ. Press, 1992.

Smith, Alice Kimball. A Peril and a Hope: The Scientists' Movement in America, 1945–47. Chicago: Univ. of Chicago Press, 1965.

Smith, Barbara Ellen. Digging our Own Graves: Coal Miners and the Struggle over Black Lung Disease. Philadelphia: Temple Univ. Press, 1987.

Smith, Merritt Roe, ed. Military Enterprise and Technological Change. Cambridge: MIT Press, 1985.

Sternglass, Ernest. Secret Fallout: Low-level Radiation from Hiroshima to Three-Mile Island. New York: McGraw-Hill, 1981.

Stone, Robert S. Industrial Medicine on the Plutonium Project. New York: McGraw-Hill, 1951.

Takaki Ronald. Double Victory: A Multicultural History of America in World War II. Boston: Little, Brown, 2000.

Tomlins, Christopher. The State and the Unions: Labor Relations, Law, and the Organized Labor Movement in America, 1880–1960. Cambridge: Cambridge Univ. Press, 1985.

U.S. Congress. Joint Committee on Atomic Energy. Labor Policy in Atomic Energy Plants. Washington, D.C.: Government Printing Office, 1948.

U.S. Department of Energy. Linking Legacies: Connecting the Cold War Nuclear Weapons Production Process to their Environmental Consequences. Washington, D.C.: Government Printing Office, 1997.

Vaughan, Diana. The Challenger Launch Decision: Risky Technology, Culture and Deviance at NASA. Chicago: Univ. of Chicago, 1996.

Walker, J. Samuel. Containing the Atom: Nuclear Regulation in a Changing Environment. Berkeley and Los Angeles: Univ. of California Press, 1992.

———. Permissible Dose: A History of Radiation Protection in the Twentieth Century. Berkeley and Los Angeles: Univ. of California Press, 2000.

Weart, Spencer. Nuclear Fear: A History of Images. Cambridge: Harvard Univ. Press, 1988.

Wendell Cultice. Youth's Battle for the Ballot. Westport, Conn.: Greenwood Press, 1992.

Whittemore, Gilbert. "The National Committee on Radiation Protection, 1928–1960." Ph.D. diss., History of Science, Harvard Univ., 1986.

Zieger, Robert. The CIO, 1935–1955. Chapel Hill: Univ. of North Carolina Press, 1995.

Index

absenteeism, 30
Advisory Committee on Human
    Radiation Experiments, 49
American Federation of Labor, 29, 83,
    93, 99, 100, 101, 103, 109, 110
Anderson, James, 16
arrests, 44–45
Atomic Energy Commission, 6, 104,
    105, 106, 107, 108, 118, 119, 120,
    127, 128
Atomic Worker, 85, 89, 90, 91, 92,
    93, 98

Barrett, James, 86, 94, 96, 97
Bates, Albert, 131
Bittner, Van, 98, 108
Black, Colleen, 16, 47
Brown v. Board of Education of
    Topeka, Kansas (1954), 114

Cade, Ebb, 49, 50, 56
Carbide   and   Carbon   Chemical
Corporation, 14, 77, 85, 87, 95, 100, 101,
106, 108, 109, 110, 117
Carr, Leslie, 37
Casper, John, 114
Center, Clark, 95
Chamberlain, Charles, 9
Chicago Defender, 74–75
Christopher, Paul, 87, 108
Clinton Engineer Works, 1
Clinton, William, 135
Cohn, Waldo, 54, 56, 114
Cole, Leonard, 54
compartmentalization, 41
Congress of Industrial Organizations,
    83, 84, 87, 90, 92, 99, 100, 101
Crawford, Lee, 23

DallaValla, J. M., 61, 63
Demeo, Esther, 92
Doyle, Charles, 94

E Awards, 65, 67
Earle, Wilton Rhodes, 109
Edwards, Alice, 73
Edwards, John, 72
Ekhalm, Sven, 32
Evans, Oliver, 16
Evans, Ophus, 86

Fair Employment Practices
    Commission, 21
Federal Bureau of Investigation, 107
Federal Mediation and Conciliation
    Service, 77
Finneran, J. A. 74
Firemen and Oilers International
    Brotherhood, 77, 78
Ford, Bacon and Davis Co., 117

Garrison, Lloyd, 106
George, Jerry, 113
Gerstle, Gary, 5
Gofman, John, 129
Goldberg, Stanley, 8
Googe, George, 96
Green Connie, 15
Green William, 86
Groves, Leslie, 1, 10, 12, 28, 29, 30,
    69, 94

Hacker, Barton, 7
Hale, Peter Bacon, 7
Hall, Helen, 18
Hanford, Washington, 81, 136
Hartfield, Harvey, 16

At Work in the Atomic City was designed and typeset on a Macintosh computer system using QuarkXPress software. The body text is set in 10.25/13 Minion and display type is set in Bernhard Modern. This book was designed and typeset by Ellen Beeler and manufactured by Thomson-Shore, Inc.